BEFORE OUR TIME

Alvan Fisher's view of Brattleboro, 1830.

BEFORE OUR TIME

A Pictorial Memoir
of Brattleboro, Vermont
From 1830 to 1930

Harold A. Barry   Richard E. Michelman   Richard M. Mitchell   Richard H. Wellman

The Stephen Greene Press : Brattleboro : Vermont

THIS BOOK IS DEDICATED
TO
ALL THE BRATTLEBORO PHOTOGRAPHERS
WITHOUT WHOSE EFFORTS IT
WOULD NOT HAVE BEEN POSSIBLE

Published December 3, 1974
Second printing, September 1979

Copyright © 1974 by Harold A. Barry, Richard E. Michelman, Richard M. Mitchell and Richard H. Wellman.

All rights reserved. No part of this book may be reproduced without written permission from the publisher, except by a reviewer who may quote brief passages or reproduce illustrations in a review; nor may any part of this book be reproduced, stored in a retrieval system, or transmitted in any form or by any means electronic, mechanical, photocopying, recording, or other, without written permission from the publisher. This book has been produced in the United States of America. It is designed by R. L. Dothard Associates, Guilford, Vt. The endpaper map of Brattleboro is by Robert MacLean of Westminster, Vt., and the jacket design is by W. Kenneth Frederick of East Thetford, Vt. The publisher of *Before Our Time* is The Stephen Greene Press of Brattleboro.

Library of Congress Cataloging in Publication Data
Main entry under title:
Before our time.
   "Limited edition of five hundred
     copies."
   Bibliography: p.
   Includes index.
   1. Brattleboro, Vt.—History—Pictorial works.
I. Barry, Harold A., 1917–   II. Title.
F59.B8B33 1974 917.43′9 74–23552
ISBN 0-8289-0215-1
ISBN 0-8289-0214-3 lim. ed.
ISBN 0-8289-0216-X pbk.

William Brattle by John Singleton Copley.

Contents

To Begin With	6
Main Street Classics	16
Fire and Flood	32
Rebuilding	40
Victorian Heyday	54
Good Times	80
A New Century	102
Just Before Our Time	135
More About the Pictures	150
Chronology	156
Other Reading	157
Index	159

TO BEGIN WITH

This book came about because the four of us—all Brattleboro-raised, one retired, two still in business, and the youngest a recent member of the history department of the high school—have long been fascinated with the past of the town, and for many years have been collecting pictures of it. The first more or less formal showing from any of our collections was in 1967, when Mr. and Mrs. Harold Barry created their slide talk, "Our Town." Then several years ago at the invitation of Librarian Eva Leech, we all lectured on local history, and subsequently participated in giving a course in local history sponsored by Vermont Community College. Finally, it was in response to growing interest that we felt we should put between covers the best of the fine pictures which show what life was like in

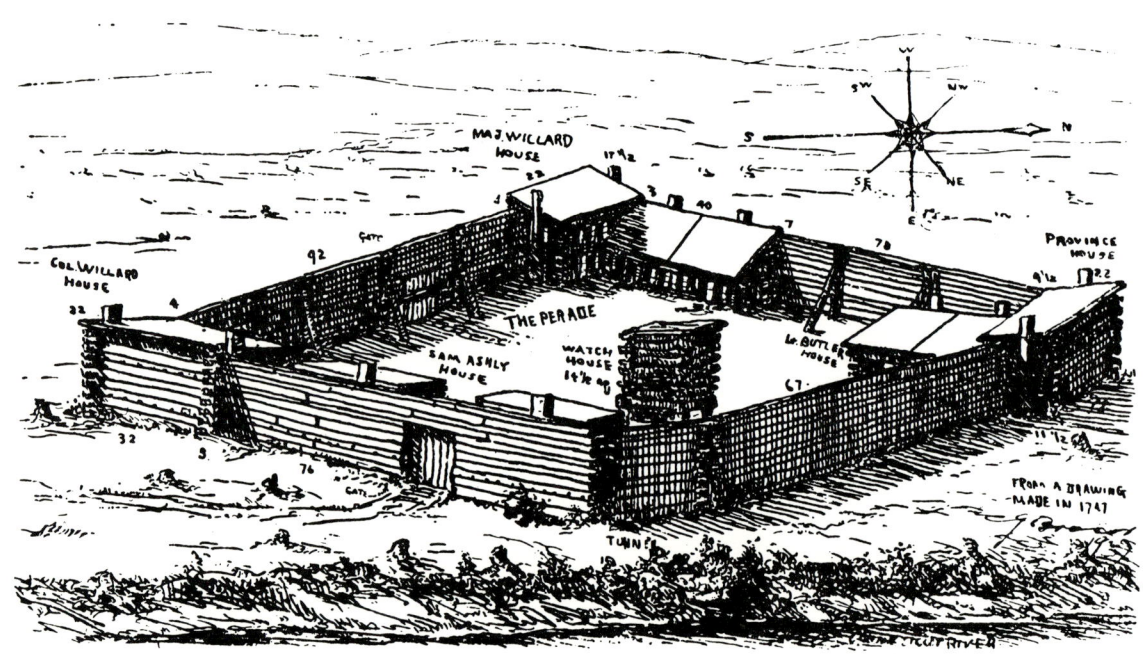

i. Fort Dummer.

Brattleboro before our time, and to this end we must have examined five thousand photographs in order to select the nearly three hundred offered here.

It was a very different town a century and a quarter ago: in most ways a lovelier town, as witness the frontispiece and the picture on Page 14. The former, the first known view of Brattleboro, was made in 1830; and it is a painting, for photography did not come to this corner of Vermont until the 1850's, when the first camera picture of the town would be made. Thereafter and until the 1900's almost all the photographs would be taken by professionals, because the equipment was both cumbersome and expensive (certainly it is no accident that photographic studios are shown in the background of a number of the early street scenes). Furthermore, since it was not yet the era of the camera, the pictures with figures were mostly posed—but to us this deliberateness increases, rather than lessens, their impact.

Aside from the need to make choices, our severest handicap lay in the fact that this was to be a *picture* book. If it were merely text, with photographs as illustrations, we could look up information we lacked and then set it down. With a picture book, though, we are limited by what artists and cameramen of the past thought were worthy subjects to commemorate. Would that we could go back in time and assign a photographer to cover a Brattleboro event that we now recognize as important or picturesque!—perhaps the Main Street fire of 1869 in

ii. The Arms Tavern.

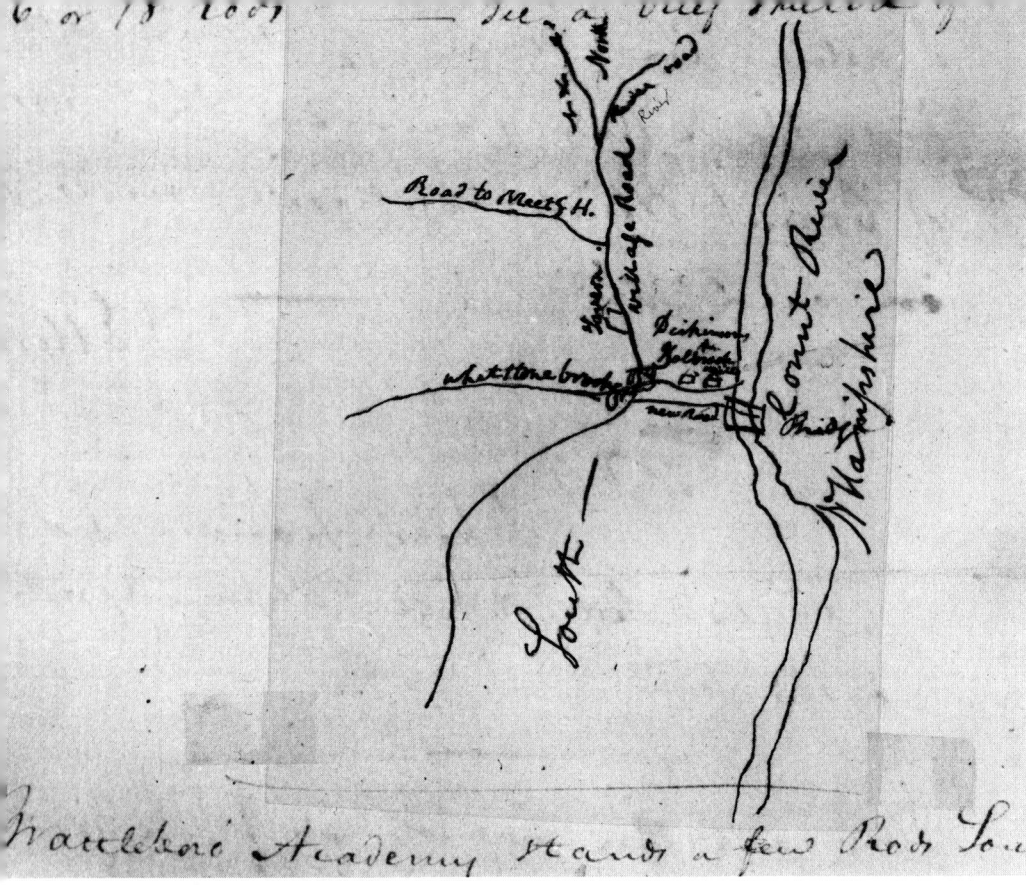

iii. Brattleboro East Village, 1810.

iv. Meeting House Hill Cemetery.

progress; or the funeral cortège of Jim Fisk winding its way up Prospect Hill; or Perry Howe and a friend going off the Harris Hill ski jump on a toboggan in the early '30s.

And of course some of the pictures that we know were taken have been lost—or at least have eluded our search. Several people in Brattleboro recall a photograph of "Farmer" Bailey lifting in the air a horse belonging to his employer of the day, a feat he was pleased to repeat on more than one occasion; but we have been unable to locate it. We are sure there are others that would have merited a place in this book, and which will surface only after publication date when it is too late. If any such pictures come to light, we shall be most grateful for the chance to examine them. Also, because of limitations of space, we could not include all the pictures we did have at hand, so there are not, for examples, every school, every church, every leading citizen. We have not been all-inclusive and we make no claim that this is the last word on the subject.

A number of the pictures will be familiar. This is especially true of most of the ones accompanying this foreword, which represent the years before the advent of the camera and which will be recognized by those who know their *Annals of Brattleboro*. In the main body of the book, starting on Page 16, we have tried to reflect the story of our town and its people—and the changes perhaps in both. We can see from the photographs that much of Brattleboro's former beauty has been destroyed, and we can infer that, in its less hectic years, the people had more time to live gently, finding more to savor in their quiet happenings and their friendships. But it is still a very good town, one with a character molded by its past, and we love it.

BEFORE OUR TIME has been a community-wide undertaking. So many families and individuals in and outside Brattleboro have contributed substantially to the making of it that we despair of including them all by name. We have, to be sure, attempted to list, in the "More About the Pictures" chapter starting on Page 150, those trusting friends and neighbors who lent us many of the prints here reproduced. To them, and to others whose names may inadvertently have been omitted, we extend a heartfelt Thank You: this book is a reality today because of their generosity.

We also want to express appreciation to a wide spectrum of special contributors: Mrs. Harold A. Barry, Miss Rachael Bodine, Judge Ralph Chapman, Charles Ebbighausen, Albert Hall, Mrs. Fred Harris, Richard Harris, Mrs. Clayton L. Hastings, James C. Irish, Robert Knowlton, Mr. and Mrs. Ralph W. Michelman, Mrs. Richard M. Mitchell, Barrows Mussey, Ralph W. Newell, Wallace Powers, Mrs. George Robbins, Norman Runnion and Staff of The *Brattleboro Reformer,* and Mrs. Richard H. Wellman and Mrs. Ralph A. Yeaw for further help with pictures; to the Vose Galleries of Boston, Inc., Allan Seymour of Vermont Studio, and especially to Lewis R. Brown, Inc., for able and patient photographic processing; to Andrew S. Kull and Castle Freeman for adroit help with the running commentary; to the Vermont Historical Society of Montpelier, Peter Thomas of the University of Massachusetts faculty, Anthony Broom of the Brattleboro Union High School faculty, and Colonel John A. Wil-

Stage Establishment.

The Proprietors of the Boston, Leominster and Brattleborough
MAIL STAGES,

TAKE this method to inform their Customers and the Public, that they continue to run a Stage as follows:—Leaves Boston every Wednesday and Saturday at 4 o'clock A. M. and arrives at Athol the same evening; returning, leaves Athol every Thursday and Monday at 4 o'clock A. M. and arrives at Boston same evening from Athol to Brattleborough. Leaves Athol every Thursday and Sunday at 6 o'clock, A. M. and arrives at Brattleborough same day at noon; returning, leaves Brattleborough every Wednesday and Sunday at 12 o'clock at noon, and arrives at Athol the same evening.

Towns through which it passes—Cambridge, West-Cambridge, Lexington, Lincoln, Concord, Acton, Stow, Bolton, Lancaster, Leominster, Fitchburg, Westminster, Gardner, Templeton, Gerry, and Athol—from thence every Thursday through Orange, Warwick, Northfield and Hinsdale to Brattleborough—and on Sunday through Orange, Warwick and Winchester to Brattleborough.

Places of Refreshment.

Concord, HAMILTON'S, Leominster, CUMMINGS'S, Westminster, DOTY'S, Athol, FIELD'S.

TRASK & DAGGETT,
PEABODY & DRAKE,
ASA W. RAND,
WILLIAM MOORE,
ARAD CHANDLER.

Each Passenger will be allowed to carry 20 lbs. gratis—120 lbs. equal to a Passenger. Every attention will be paid to baggage, but at the risque of the owner.

N. B. For Seats, apply at Mrs. TRASK'S, sign of the Indian Queen, Bromfield's-lane, Boston.
JANUARY 10, 1815.

v. Stagecoach line schedule.

liams, Editor of State Papers, Montpelier, for valued historical contributions. Mrs. Eva Leech and Staff of the Brooks Memorial Library have been especially co-operative—and forbearing, in view of our continual demands on their time and energy.

Finally we thank Mr. and Mrs. F. Cabot Holbrook and Mr. and Mrs. Hyacinth Renaud for having unreservedly put at our disposal, as the credits in the back of the book attest, a virtually unlimited amount of material from their collections. And we are boundlessly grateful to Howard C. Rice, Jr., who has not only generously shared his time and experience to keep this book on course, but whose ingenious sleuthing in our behalf has yielded many other plums, notably the first known view of the town, the Alvan Fisher painting; and to Mr. and Mrs. Renouf Russell, of Russell Wesselhoeft Farm, Jaffrey, New Hampshire, who most kindly made the Fisher painting available to us and have permitted us to reproduce it.

Our credits would not be complete if we did not mention the late Lewis R. Brown, the foremost collector of photographic Brattleboreana. This book, like other historical projects in the area during the past half-century, owes much to his enthusiasm, foresight, and generosity.

vi. Royall Tyler.

Brattleboro is what it is because of the lie of the land and because of the passions of the people who lived here in centuries gone by. The geography is never taken into account nowadays, unless it is to hail the town as the southeastern gateway to the beckoning Green Mountains and their recreation areas; the passions have been forgotten. But our town would be very different now if it were not for these two factors.

To average people like us, geological history is hard to grasp. We are told that shallow seas washed this area 460 million years ago, and that later convulsions raised and let drop the crust of earth, twisting it into new shapes and drowning it in molten lava; and finally the torment ceased, leaving the land to erode for nearly 300 million years of comparative stability. Then, in a time the geologists think of as yesterday, a blanket of ice several thousands of feet thick spread over New England, in some places buffing high land into gentle contours, in others dumping monster loads of glacial débris lugged down from the north.

Finally, when the ice melted some 30,000 years ago, the land that emerged was shaped much as it is today. The arrival and departure of the Great Ice Age is still attested dramatically by a "kettle pond" to the northwest of the present Union High School; this depression, about the size of a football stadium, was formed when a huge ice block left behind by the glacier thawed at last, leaving nothing to support its rocky cover of insulation. Less casually intriguing but of incalculable importance in shaping the town and its people is another legacy from the eons of geological cataclysms—and this is the Connecticut River.

From its headwaters in the Connecticut Lakes near the Canadian border, the great stream flows, benignly in most seasons, past Brattleboro, set roughly at the midpoint of its progress due south toward Long Island Sound. It is the eastern boundary of town—indeed of the State of Vermont—and from the hills of Brattleboro near its shoreline one looks across the river spang into the face of the somber tree-clad height of land that is Wantastiquet Mountain in New Hampshire. Long before it was a boundary, however, it was an artery that brought travelers up from the flatter, more populous lands to the south.

Even in local prehistory there were few permanent settlements along the river around present-day Brattleboro. True, there are signs of Indian habitations as long ago as 10,000 to 8,500 B.C.; and petroglyphs, now underwater where the West River debouches into the Connecticut at the north end of town, and innumerable artifacts and arrowpoints unearthed in the area, give proof of the active Indian life in and around the town. But most of this life in more recent times was migratory; the Pocumtucks and the Squakeags are the best known of these early transients. Now only Wantastiquet across the river, the Connecticut

vii. Deacon John Holbrook.   **viii.** Mrs. John Holbrook.

itself, Wicopee Hill, and Indian Flat, where this book is published, pay place-name tribute to the first inhabitants.

The land around town was then a wilderness, but a generous one, with the skies full of birds and the dense forests full of game, and the big river alive with shad and salmon. Mary R. Cabot, in her *Annals of Brattleboro, 1681–1895*, relays an anonymous report of 1803 that in spawning season the mouth of the West River contained so many salmon "that it looked as if one could walk across from one shore to the other." The earliest white visitors were probably also hunters and trappers, for if you were a capable man on water or in the woods there was no danger that you would starve.

The last quarter of the seventeenth century saw people starting to homestead in the Connecticut Valley not far below Brattleboro, and almost coincidentally began successive tugs-of-war that would plague our area for the next hundred years.

The first long-drawn strife, created by hostilities between Britain and France, was carried to the New World as the French and Indian wars, which lasted off and on from 1689 until the Treaty of Paris in 1763. The bloody Indian raid on Deerfield, only twenty-odd miles south of Brattleboro as the crow flies, was instigated by the French in 1704, and skirmishes close to home continued for the next decade. It was during a comparative lull in 1718 that the land which is Brattleboro was bought at auction for around one farthing an acre by a group of Bay State notables that included William Dummer, Lieutenant-Governor of Massachusetts, and William Brattle of Cambridge (who was never to see the town to which his name was given). The parcel of land so acquired was called, initially, Dummerston, and on it was built in 1724 a blockhouse to protect the settlers of valley communities farther south.

Thus did Fort Dummer become the first permanent British settlement in what is now Vermont; it was the birthplace, in 1726, of Timothy Dwight, the first white child known to have been born in the state. An active post for only a few years, its site is just south of the present Erving Paper plant—under water backed up by the dam downriver at Vernon.

ix. Dr. John Wilson—"Thunderbolt"?

The Indians continued raiding the area sporadically for the next three decades, marching their captives north to the French in Canada; then came the fall of Quebec to the British in 1759 to mark the end of fighting in the struggle between France and Great Britain for control of North

America. It should also have marked the beginning of a trouble-free era for the settlers putting down roots in Brattleboro. But it didn't. A mere five years later a decree by George III started a wrangle among the town's residents that would breed a bitterness lasting until after the Revolution was fought and won.

In 1753 Benning Wentworth, Governor of New Hampshire, had issued a royal grant for land within the present boundaries of our town, naming it Brattleborough. It was not Wentworth's first grant, and it was far from his last, for he issued so many—covering roughly half of Vermont—that the region became known as the Hampshire Grants. Contentedly, then, the handful of newcomers to town were living in "the Grants" when the King acceded in 1764 to the claim of New York that its own colonial charter a century earlier had placed its eastern limits on the west bank of the Connecticut River; hence Brattleboro should be designated as in Cumberland County of the Province of New York. Faced with the prospect that their land titles were null and void, the grantees of our town sought and received a confirming patent from New York in 1766, and two years later a town meeting is recorded under the new jurisdiction.

For the next fifteen years the fires of local politics were fed by the conflicting requirements for settlement under the New Hampshire grants and the New York patents. The creation in 1777 of the republic of Vermont did nothing to help matters: it simply gave the townspeople a third

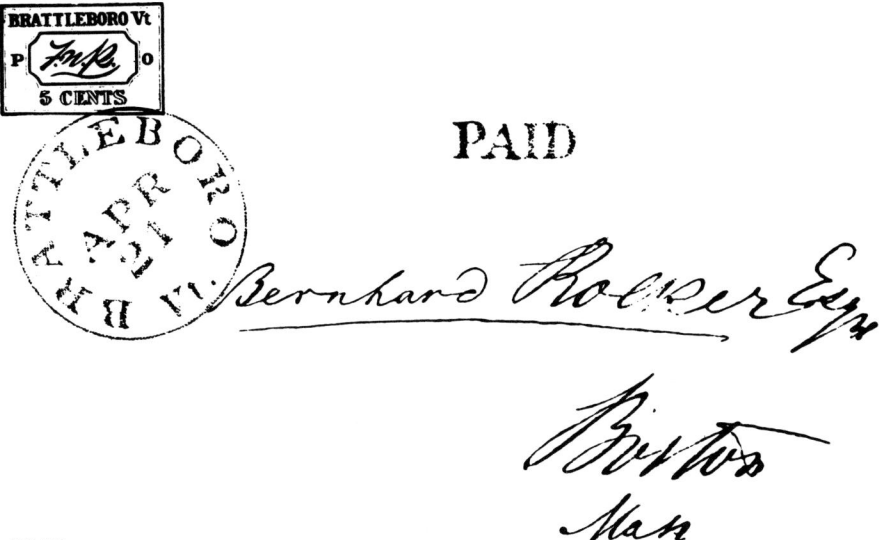

x. Brattleboro Postage Stamp, 1845.

xi. Stephan's view of Brattleboro, 1849.

America. It should also have marked the beginning of a trouble-free era for the settlers putting down roots in Brattleboro. But it didn't. A mere five years later a decree by George III started a wrangle among the town's residents that would breed a bitterness lasting until after the Revolution was fought and won.

In 1753 Benning Wentworth, Governor of New Hampshire, had issued a royal grant for land within the present boundaries of our town, naming it Brattleborough. It was not Wentworth's first grant, and it was far from his last, for he issued so many—covering roughly half of Vermont —that the region became known as the Hampshire Grants. Contentedly, then, the handful of newcomers to town were living in "the Grants" when the King acceded in 1764 to the claim of New York that its own colonial charter a century earlier had placed its eastern limits on the west bank of the Connecticut River; hence Brattleboro should be designated as in Cumberland County of the Province of New York. Faced with the prospect that their land titles were null and void, the grantees of our town sought and received a confirming patent from New York in 1766, and two years later a town meeting is recorded under the new jurisdiction.

For the next fifteen years the fires of local politics were fed by the conflicting requirements for settlement under the New Hampshire grants and the New York patents. The creation in 1777 of the republic of Vermont did nothing to help matters: it simply gave the townspeople a third

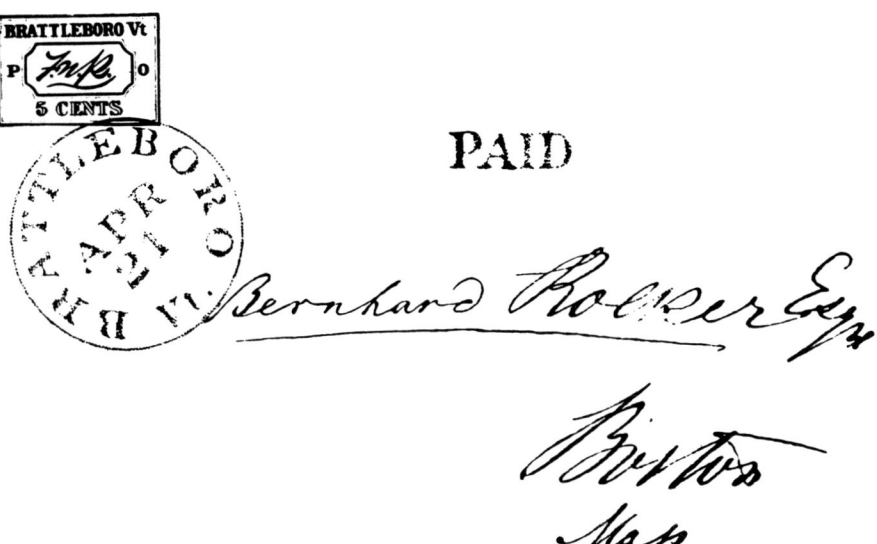

x. Brattleboro Postage Stamp, 1845.

xi. Stephan's view of Brattleboro, 1849.

option—which they rejected the following year by a 165-to-1 vote of dissent from "the pretended State of Vermont." It took Brigadier General Ethan Allen himself, riding hell-for-leather at the head of militia troops in 1782, to bring the area finally under the sole jurisdiction of Vermont. Meanwhile the American Revolution had ended.

And meanwhile Brattleboro had been building.

The earliest road in town was a former scout path from Fort Dummer to Chase's Cascade—still to be seen beside Route 142—up along Venter's Brook to the present Old Guilford Road, where it headed southwest into Massachusetts. Fairbank and Benjamin Moor turned their backs on this established trail when they left the fort to build Brattleboro's first private dwelling. They blazed a path north through the forest to the terrace of land above the location today of the Retreat farmhouse, and there they erected a log cabin in 1757. Five years later John Arms built the town's first tavern near by; it would become our first post office in 1784 under the independent republic of Vermont, with Arms as its postmaster.

However, the nucleus of the main section of Brattleboro—later to be called the "east village," as opposed to West Brattleboro—was the mills on the falls of Whetstone Brook, just above Main Street bridge. One, a gristmill, was built in 1762; Colonel Samuel Wells, the town's most ardent supporter of the New York faction, established his sawmill there in 1768. That same year saw the erection of our first meeting house, almost midway between the east and west settlements: it was on Meeting House Hill (upper Orchard Street) and was used for civil gatherings as well as for worship. Brattleboro's first store was established in 1771 by Stephen Greenleaf of Boston near where the Union Block stands today on Main Street.

Steadily, solidly Brattleboro grew, and although mills sprang up along Whetstone Brook from the "west village" to its mouth at the Connecticut, the products it shipped downriver were mainly from the land: pitch, tar and turpentine, lumber and pearl ash, flaxseed and grain, tallow and pork. In return the flatboats, offloading at the foot of what is now Arch Street, brought salt codfish, sugar, molasses, salt and spices; metalware and cloth, glass, black powder and cigars. In addition, the steamboats *Barnett*, *John Ledyard* and *William Holmes* made regular stops between 1827 and 1831.

The decade before the main body of this book begins saw the largest jump thus far in the town's population—2,623 in the 1840 Census, against 3,816 in 1850. But by then the Wesselhoeft Water Cure on Elliot Street had been attracting wealthy patrons from all over the country, Jacob Estey had established his organ factory on Main Street, and, in 1849, the first railroad train to town drew in with 1,500 passengers.

Brattleboro was coming into its own.

Harold A. Barry
Richard E. Michelman
Richard M. Mitchell
Richard H. Wellman

MAIN STREET CLASSICS

1. Brattleboro, across the Connecticut River from Wantastiquet Mountain, New Hampshire, 1856.

Pictures of Brattleboro made in the 1850's and '60's show buildings and streets that we recognize today: the village was assuming its future shape. The outside world began, occasionally, to notice Brattleboro—when people arrived to take the water cure, or read in the papers about Larkin Mead's "Snow Angel." In the difficult years of the Civil War, Vermont chose a Brattleboro man—Frederick Holbrook—to be Governor. Among many enterprises started and abandoned, a few gained hold: one was Jacob Estey's organ factory. Main Street, in wood, burned or was simply torn down, to be rebuilt in brick.

Two complementary photographs provide a composite portrait of Main Street hill in the years before the Civil War. One looks south on a summer day. It is shirtsleeve and parasol weather, although one gentleman still wears his stovepipe hat. The brand-new brick house on the left, illuminated by the afternoon sun from Flat Street, had just been put up by Anthony Van Doorn, the furniture maker. The only one of these buildings still standing, it is known today as the Culver Block. The second picture looks in the opposite direction, up the hill. It was taken from the top window in the north side of Mr. Van Doorn's house. There one sees three of Brattleboro's seven hotels: the pillared American House in the right foreground; the Revere House, with its twin chimneys, at the corner of Elliot Street; and farther along on the left (where the stagecoach waits), the Brattleboro House. Frequent stages served Townshend, Williamsville, Dover, and Hinesburg Village in Guilford. The covered wagon laboring up the hill carries freight, probably to Wilmington.

Opposite: **2.** Main Street, looking south from Elliot Street, 1853.

3. Main Street, looking north from Flat Street, 1860.

The Hydropathic System of physical therapy, popularly known as the "water cure," afforded a refined convalescence for the well-to-do of the 1850's. The most famous (and socially acceptable) water cure in America was the Elliot Street establishment of Dr. Robert Wesselhoeft, a follower of the Austrian hydropathist Priessnitz. The Brattleboro Hydropathic Institution opened its doors in 1845 and was soon doing a thriving business. This was in spite of an unfavorable notice in the *Boston Medical and Surgical Journal,* which suggested that practitioners of the water cure were in many cases fakes who took up the water cure only after they had failed in other schools of quack medicine.

Dr. Wesselhoeft's establishment had distinct attractions. In addition to every conceivable kind of bath, there were pleasant walks and gardens, picnics, archery, simple games, and dances on Wednesdays and Saturdays. These amenities induced patients to pay willingly the considerable sum of $10 weekly ($11 in summer), which made Wesselhoeft's, among its other

4. Rules of the House. **5.** Wesselhoeft's, at the corner of Church and Elliot, ca. 1850.

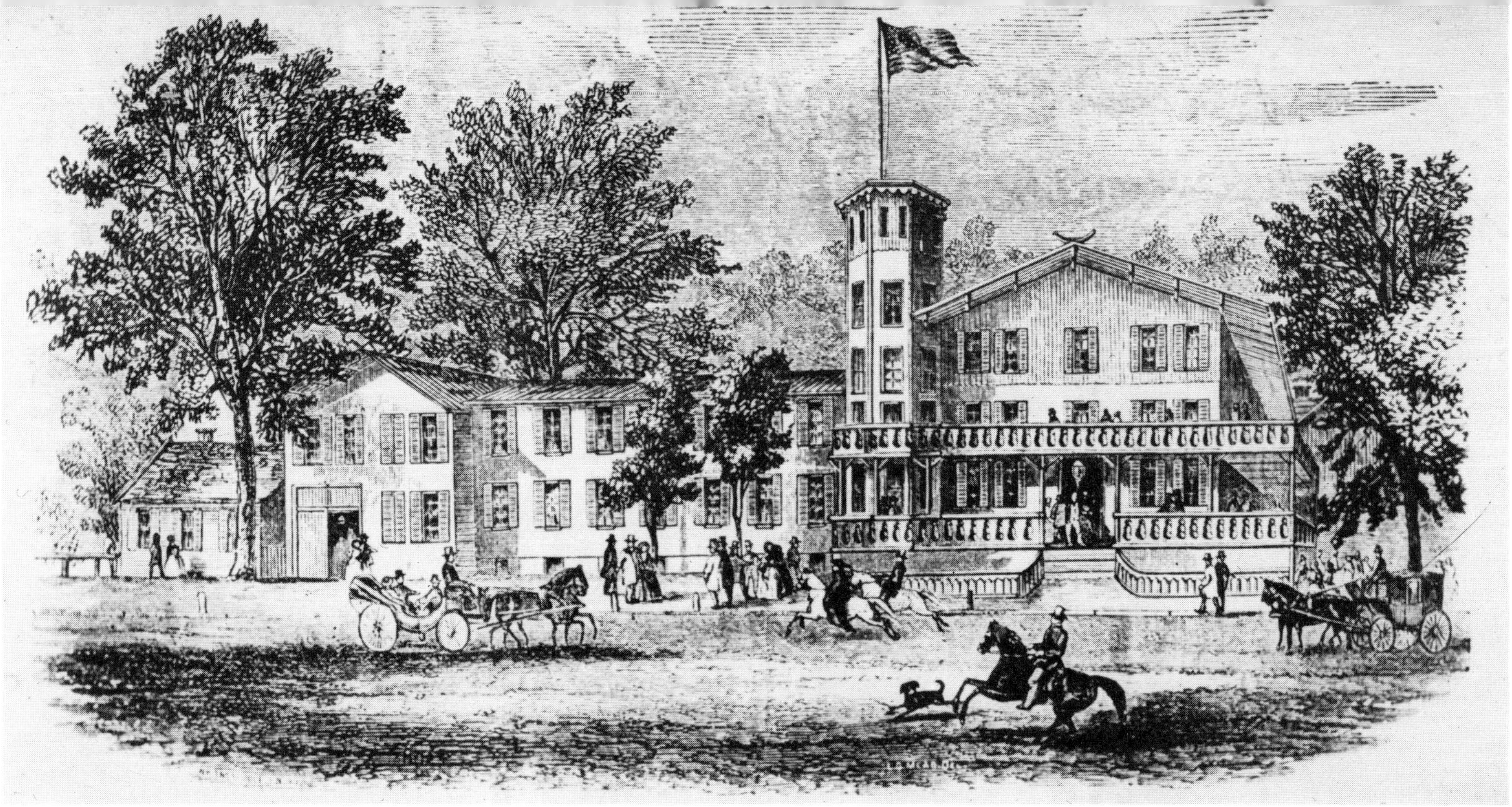

distinctions, America's most expensive cure. Many famous people came to Brattleboro for treatment: they included Harriet Beecher Stowe, Henry Wadsworth Longfellow, Francis Parkman, James Russell Lowell, and William Dean Howells. In the round of healthy pleasures, some boarders did complain of the frequent ice-cold "plunges"; others complained of the food: two of the three daily meals consisted primarily of stale bread.

Wesselhoeft's Cure stood on the site of the present-day Central Fire Station. The Lawrence Water Cure, erected directly across the street in 1853, enjoyed only a brief prosperity. It was out of business by 1860, although five years later its fine ballroom could still be engaged for an evening (**7**).

6. The rival Lawrence Water Cure, Elliot Street, 1857.

7.

Grand Masquerade Ball,

AT THE "LAWRENCE,"

MONDAY, AUGUST 28, 1865.

THIS TICKET IS NOT TRANSFERABLE.

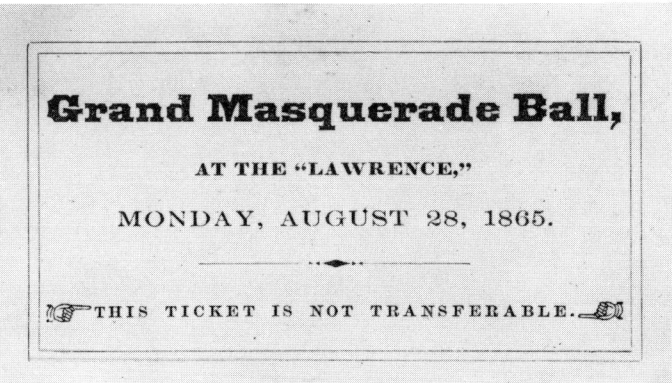

8. View down Bridge Street, to the Connecticut River and the Island, 1850's.

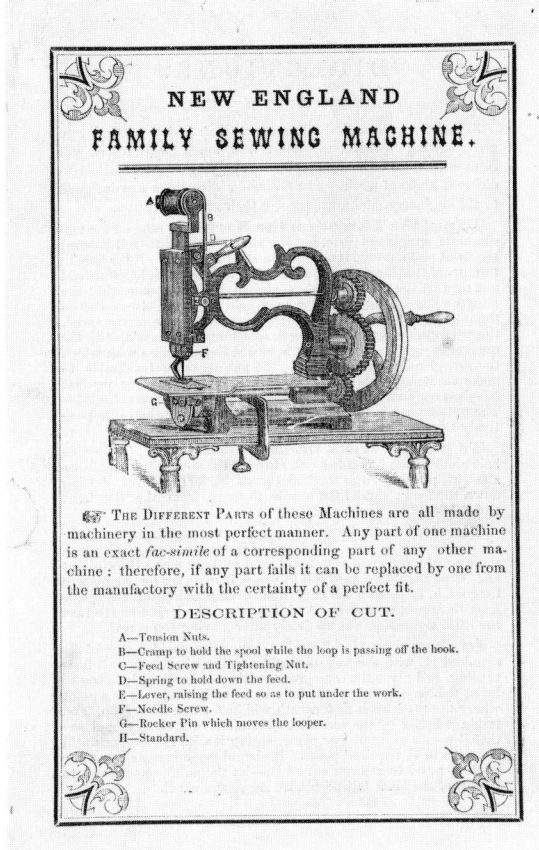

9.

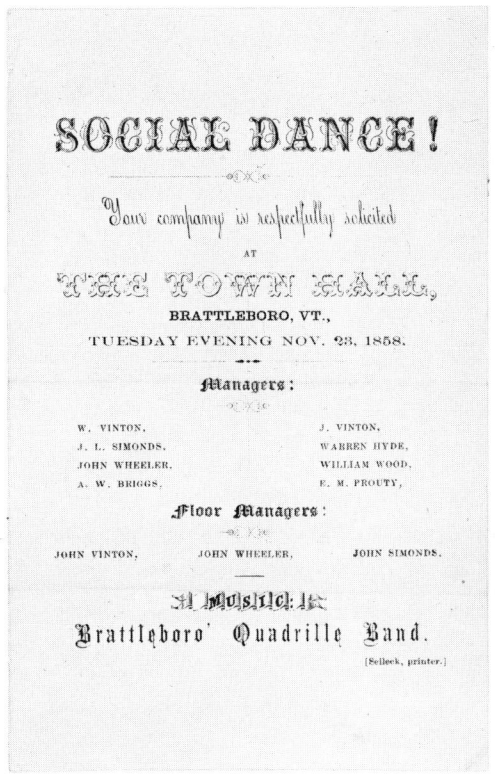

10.   **11.**

In the Bridge Street scene at left, the old flour mill occupies the present site of the Railroad Diner. The sign, LOOK OUT FOR THE ENGINE, over the tracks was a common warning in America before the invention of the standard "Stop, Look and Listen" crossbars.

Typical of Brattleboro manufactures in the decade of the Civil War was the New England Family Sewing Machine, which was made by Charles Raymond from 1859 to 1863. Over the next twenty years there were seven more attempts to manufacture sewing machines in Brattleboro—none of them very successful.

From the same period, the "managers" of the Town Hall Dance were prominent young men in the town. Most of these men would be at war within three years. John Vinton and Warren Hyde were two of Brattleboro's Civil War officers. In the handbill for Wheeler's Skates can be read the record of a local business partnership gone sour: Tyler & Thompson were successors to the business of Williston & Tyler in the long genealogy of a noted Brattleboro hardware store.

12. U.S. Military Hospital, at the south outskirts of town, 1863.

13. Military Hospital supply hut and patients.

14. Governor Frederick Holbrook.

Frederick Holbrook, born February 15, 1813, the son of Deacon John Holbrook, was one of the Brattleboro men to become Governor of Vermont. A state senator in 1849 and 1850, he served as Governor from 1861 to 1863, during the war maintaining his official residence at the Brattleboro House. In his last year in office he brought about the establishment of a United States Military Hospital on the mustering grounds that are the present site of Brattleboro Union High School. Some 4,500 soldiers from Vermont and neighboring states were treated here.

Throughout his life Holbrook was a devoted agriculturalist. His essays on farming subjects were widely reprinted, and he designed several plows and other implements—one of them, the "Holbrook Plow," was in common use for many years. From 1852 until his death in 1909, Holbrook was a trustee of the Brattleboro Retreat, where he took particular interest in overseeing the activities of the farming department.

15. Burnside Military School, 1860's.

16. Main Street Bridge over Whetstone Brook, mid-1850's.

17.

The Burnside Military School was located a mile north of the village off Upper Dummerston Road. It was founded in 1859 by Charles Miles, a young Bostonian. The building, later taken over by the Retreat, burned in 1920. Burnside attracted students from a wide area.

In the large white factory beside Whetstone Brook (at left) Anthony Van Doorn started his furniture making business in 1815. The darker building partially visible at left is the original factory of the Estey Organ Company. Both these buildings, and fourteen others, were destroyed in the fire of September 4, 1857. Another view across Whetstone Brook (**17**) shows the Brattleboro Melodeon Company. Organized in 1867, this was a short-lived rival to the Estey Organ enterprises. Behind it in the same picture is the original building of the First Baptist Church on Elliot Street. Services were held there from 1841 to 1868, when the present church was built on Main Street. The Elliot Street building was later added to, and became the Princess Hotel.

18. View west from Flat Street, 1860's.

An early photograph shows Frost Meadow and Whetstone Brook from Flat Street before the south side of the street was developed. The brick building to the left occupied the present site of the Latchis Hotel. In the distance (at the corner of Frost and Elm Streets) is one of the Estey workshops. To the right is the Frost family mansion. The wagons in the foreground probably belonged to Ray's Livery Stables, across Flat Street.

The Honorable Larkin G. Mead, himself a respected attorney, moved to Brattleboro from New Hampshire in 1839 and brought with him his exceptional family. His daughter Elinor became the wife of William Dean Howells. His fourth son, William Rutherford Mead, was a partner of McKim, Mead & White, in its time the most distinguished architectural firm in America.

It was the second son of the family, Larkin G. Mead, Jr., whose career had the closest ties to Brattleboro. A shy and retiring youth, Mead gave early evidence of a talent for sculpture when, as a twenty-one-year-old clerk for Williston & Tyler's

19. Burnham's Foundry, Main Street, 1850's.

20. The "Snow Angel."

hardware store, he produced a marble pig which caught the eye of an artist taking the water cure at Wesselhoeft's. The artist encouraged Mead to train and use his talent. After two years' study in New York, Mead returned to Brattleboro and opened a studio for drawing lessons. On New Year's Eve, 1856, he worked through the night to create an elaborate snow sculpture at the junction of Main and Linden Streets. He was assisted by Edward and Henry Burnham, who, to melt snow and thaw fingers, kept a fire going in their brass foundry (**19**), which was nearby on the present site of Brooks Memorial Library. Mead produced the figure of a Recording Angel, eight feet high, as a New Year's display for the village. The "Snow Angel" was an immense success. Mead received admiring press notices and several commissions, including one for a marble copy of the Angel. A successful career followed, in the course of which Mead produced major works, including a statue of Ethan Allen for the State House in Montpelier and the Lincoln tomb in Springfield, Illinois. Brattleboro, too, can boast a characteristic example of his work: the Jim Fisk monument in Prospect Hill Cemetery.

21. At the intersection of Main and High Streets looking south, 1860's.

22. At the intersection of Elliot and

Three photographs give a close-up view of the east side of Main Street at a time when the smaller wooden buildings were giving way to the brick "blocks" that stand there today. Between High and Elliot streets the retail establishments on the east side of Main Street provided a nearly unbroken line of sidewalk roofs and awnings, with merchandise set out front. In the background of (**21**) is, once again, Mr. Van Doorn's solid brick house, known today

Main, looking north, 1860's.

23. Main Street, from the end of Elliot, ca. 1853.

as the Culver Block. Plate 22 looks north toward the spire of the Congregational Church. The portrait of the Cutler and Exchange blocks (**23**) was probably taken by the daguerreotypist whose shingle hangs above the third story. The white frame building housing the bookstore was demolished about 1861 and replaced by the Union Block.

31

VT. RECORD AND FARMER.

EXTRA.

WEDNESDAY, OCTOBER 6, 1869.

THE VERMONT RECORD AND FARMER
F. D. COBLEIGH,
Editor and Publisher.
Published every Friday in Brattleboro, Vt.
Terms: 2.50 per year, always in advance. Single copies 8 cents.

THE FLOOD!

Immense Destruction of Property.

LOSS, FULLY $300,000.

WHETSTONE CREEK BRIDGE GONE.

Brook Road Washed Completely Out!

TWO LIVES LOST!

Connecticut River Toll Bridge Gone.

As Public Journalists it devolves upon us to chronicle the most fearful devastation of property and great exertion, the family were all gotten out alive and the sick lady was given a resting place for her weary head at the house of Mrs. Whitney, on Elliot-st. Mr. Elliot, also residing on this street, had a sister sick at his house. She was taken out alive and found refuge at the house of Mr. Green, on Elliot-st. A small house situated near the aqueduct was half submerged, the brick foundation was gullied out for nearly the whole length of one side of the house, and naught but a miracle saved the slender fabric from going off without leave or license. The house of Willard Frost, on the lower side of the street, was in a peculiarly exposed situation. The fences were broken down by the ferocity of the current, the wood shed was veered around, the barn was shaken on its foundation, and inevitable destruction seemed imminent. The house was occupied by the female members of Mr. Frost's family, together with Mr. Eugene Frost, Mr. Wells Frost and his mother. They all went to the upper chamber of the house and there made signals of distress from the windows to the assembled multitude on Elliot-st. The rapid current which eddied and whirled around dam. Ropes are thrown to him, they cannot reach him, he makes no effort to save himself. He is now just on the verge of the dam at the northern edge. If he jumps he may yet be saved. He is entreated so to do with a wild shout from the bystanders, he throws his hands aloft and with one wild, despairing look goes over into the seething whirlpool, into eternity. For a second every one is transfixed with horror, then the wildest excitement prevails. Men rush frantically after boats with the vague hope of saving him at the river. Futile, however, were all efforts, as the poor man's body must have been horribly mutilated and at once floated into the Connecticut. Mr. Fredericks was a poor man and leaves a wife and five children. Fredericks was one of three survivors out of 700 who were lost at the wrecking of the steam ship Central America several years ago, and it seems a strange fatality that he should have been spared at that time only to meet such a terrible fate here and find a watery grave at last. Poor fellow, he is gone, and in all probability his body will never be recovered, although every effort is being made to get it if possible. Let us one and all

rapidity with which this wholesale dissolution took place can be conveyed by words. The magician's "now you see it, and now you don't." was amply illustrated.

NEWMAN AND TYLER'S MACHINE SHOP.

About 100 feet to the rear of Main-st., on the north side of the creek, stands a large brick building, built upon a solid rock foundation, owned and occupied by Newman & Tyler as a machine shop. Nearly simultaneous with the crash and rush of the large bodies mentioned above, the entire wall on the brook side of this building fell in the water with a "thud." The immense weight of the lathes on the floors caused them to sag considerably; the machinery was soon moved to the sound side of the building, however, and it sustained no further damage. The theory of the dropping of this wall is that the flume was connected with and built into the main wall, and becoming choked up with large timbers some heavy body struck them and using them as levers, pried the wall off its equilibrium and over it went. The loss of this firm is quite heavy, the stoppage of their business being very detrimental.

FIRE AND FLOOD

The 1860's brought three local disasters to Brattleboro. On April 17, 1862, an unseasonably warm day melted the deep snow in the Connecticut River valley. The resulting flood reduced at one stroke the area of Brattleboro's Island from twenty-two to eight acres. Far greater damage to the business district resulted from the flood of October 4, 1869. Rain began to fall on October 2 and continued un-

25. The Island's bridges survive the flood of 1862.

interrupted for thirty-six hours. This time most of the destruction was wrought by normally peaceful Whetstone Brook, which swept away every one of its bridges between the covered span in West Brattleboro and the railroad bridge at the Connecticut.

On October 31, a fire broke out in A. E. Eayer's Eating Saloon and destroyed all the buildings on the west side of Main Street between High and Elliot. The fire was fanned by a strong wind, and fire fighting efforts were hampered by effects of the recent flood. In particular, the flood having destroyed the Main Street Bridge, the South Main Street company could not get to the fire quickly. Fortunately, no lives were lost.

While the flood of 1862 did its main damage to the Island, the 1869 flood knocked out both the Connecticut River and Main Street bridges and undermined buildings on both sides of Whetstone Brook. The covered bridge to the Island (**26**) was in fact destroyed by the force of water from the Brook, rather than by the Connecticut itself. The building at the far end of the bridge is the span's tollhouse; the building in the left foreground is on the present site of the Allen Oil Company. The Hines, Newman machine shop (**27**), on Arch Street east of Main, was ripped open by Whetstone Brook, exposing the two water wheels in its basement. One wheel powered the shop machinery; the other was used to pump water for fire fighting into underground cisterns in the business district of the village. This water was sorely missed when fire struck soon after the flood.

The view to the west up Whetstone Brook (**28**) shows a number of men enjoying the fall sunshine directly underneath the former span of Main Street Bridge. Standing somewhat precariously to the left is one of the Estey buildings; in the far right background is the Frost mansion. The view up Main Street from the southern end of the vanished bridge (**29**) gives an idea of the process of reconstruction after the fire and flood. The indestructible brick building to the right is the Van Doorn house.

26. East from Bridge Street, October 1869.

27. Machine shop on Whetstone Brook, October 1869.

28. Whetstone Brook without Main Street Bridge, 1869.

29. Main Street Bridge, October 1869.

30. Blake Block, northwest corner of Main and Elliot streets, 1860.

again
...disaster

The fire of October 31st razed all the buildings on the west side of Main Street between High and Elliot. One of the casualties was the striking Blake Block (**30**). Originally a fine private house, by 1822 an inn, and finally converted to retail shopfronts, it continued to maintain a dignified appearance. (Notice the flagstone crosswalks at the muddy intersection.) The Revere House stables were in the white building with a cupola. Another disastrous fire began in these stables in 1877 and destroyed the Revere House. The Elliot Street Methodist Church, now a community theater, was erected on the site of the stables.

31. Main Street, west side, High to Elliot, October 1869.

32. Brattleboro House, west side of Main Street, halfway between Elliot and High, 1860's.

The Brattleboro House had seen its palmiest days when it was consumed by the October fire. In former times, as "Chase's Stage House," it had been the junction of major long-distance stage routes from Boston, Troy, Hanover, and Hartford. After the coming of the railroads, Brattleboro was never again such an important crossroads, though the Brattleboro House remained a center of social life in the village and the stopping point for the local Windham County stages. A picture taken from across the street (**33**) shows the site after the fire: the livery stables and other buildings in back were unharmed. In front of the deep foundations of the Blake Block, the remains of shopfronts and hitching posts can just be recognized from the earlier photograph (**30**).

33. Site of Blake Block and Brattleboro House after the fire.

REBUILDING

Brattleboro's great fire of 1869 provided an occasion for rebuilding. The Brooks House and the Crosby Block filled the gap on Main Street and gave to the business district much of the look it has today. The great civic and social organizations of the day were the volunteer fire companies. In the years that followed the fire they grew in resources and in show. And a brilliant son of Brattleboro, "Jubilee Jim" Fisk, appeared to dazzle the nation.

34. Buddington's gristmill, Bridge Street, 1870's.

The mill on Bridge Street by the railroad tracks (**34,** also visible in **8**) was built in 1832. Before Buddington & Brother took it over as a flour mill it had been used, among other things, as a tannery, a planing mill, and a melodeon factory. One of the building's tenants was John Gore, the machinist who made Brattleboro's contribution to the development of the automobile. Between 1835 and 1837—perhaps in this building—Gore designed and built a self-propelled wagon. Powered by a steam boiler and a two cylinder engine, the wagon could go fifteen miles per hour.

35. Centerville Mill, Western Avenue at Williams Street, ca. 1930.

36.

Like Buddington's Mill, the Centerville Mill—shown here (**35**) just before its demolition in the 1930's—had many and varied tenants. In 1865 a furniture factory occupied the building, and in 1879 a knitting machine manufacturing company took it over (**36**). After that the mill housed an electrical generator and later, for a time, a roller skating rink. By the 1920's the mill's tenants were small businessmen once more: Shaw's cider mill, Avery's barrel shop, and Birch's rug factory.

41

37. William Morris Hunt, 1870's.

38. "The Prodigal Son," Brooks Memorial Library.

Like the Meads, the Hunts were a Brattleboro family of unusual accomplishment. William Morris Hunt, born in Brattleboro in 1824, studied painting in Paris and later pursued a successful career in Boston until his death by drowning in 1879. "The Prodigal Son," much admired when he painted it in Paris, was exhibited by invitation in New York and New Haven, where unfriendly critics suggested that the work showed "what could be done with a trowel." The painting hangs today in the Brooks Library, a bequest of Hunt's sister.

Hunt's younger brother, Richard Morris Hunt, designed the Washington Naval Observatory, the original Fogg Museum at Harvard, and the pedestal for the Statue of Liberty. He also designed two of the Vanderbilt family's celebrated houses: the "Breakers," in Newport, R.I.; and "Biltmore," in Asheville, N.C.

39. Hayes Tavern, West Brattleboro.

40.

Rutherford Hayes, grandfather of the nineteenth President of the United States, came to West Brattleboro in 1778, married a local girl, and decided to stay. He built the inn which was later known as Hayes Tavern, and had his name painted over a secondhand sign to hang outside. With fourteen fireplaces and a ballroom, the Tavern was the center of social activities in the region. The Hayes Tavern was torn down in 1960; part of its site is now the parking lot of the State Liquor Store.

41. Elliot, School, and Green streets, 1870's.

A panoramic view from Birge Street (**41**) shows part of residential Brattleboro in the 1870's. In the foreground is Elliot Street; behind it, Green Street. School Street runs uphill to the right. The brick building on School Street housed the Methodist Church before the construction of the church on Elliot Street in 1880. The old church remains today as an apartment house. George Jones Brooks built his Brooks House (**42**) soon after the site at Main and High Streets was left vacant by the 1869 fire. It remains the handsomest building in Brattleboro, even without the porch and colonnade on the east side, which have been removed. The work of rebuilding the burned out section of Main Street is partially visible in (**43**), where oxen are moving a building down Elliot Street past the construction site of the Crosby Block. The beautiful elm tree at the corner of the Blake Block (**30**) was destroyed in the fire; its pulled stump is visible in the foreground here.

The bulky equipment needed to photograph these scenes of early Brattleboro was moved around in pushcarts (**44**).

42.

43.

44.

45. Crosby Block under construction, Main Street, 1870.

46. Edward Crosby.

47. Willard's store in the Crosby Block, ca. 1890.

48. Crosby mill, Bridge Street, ca. 1910.

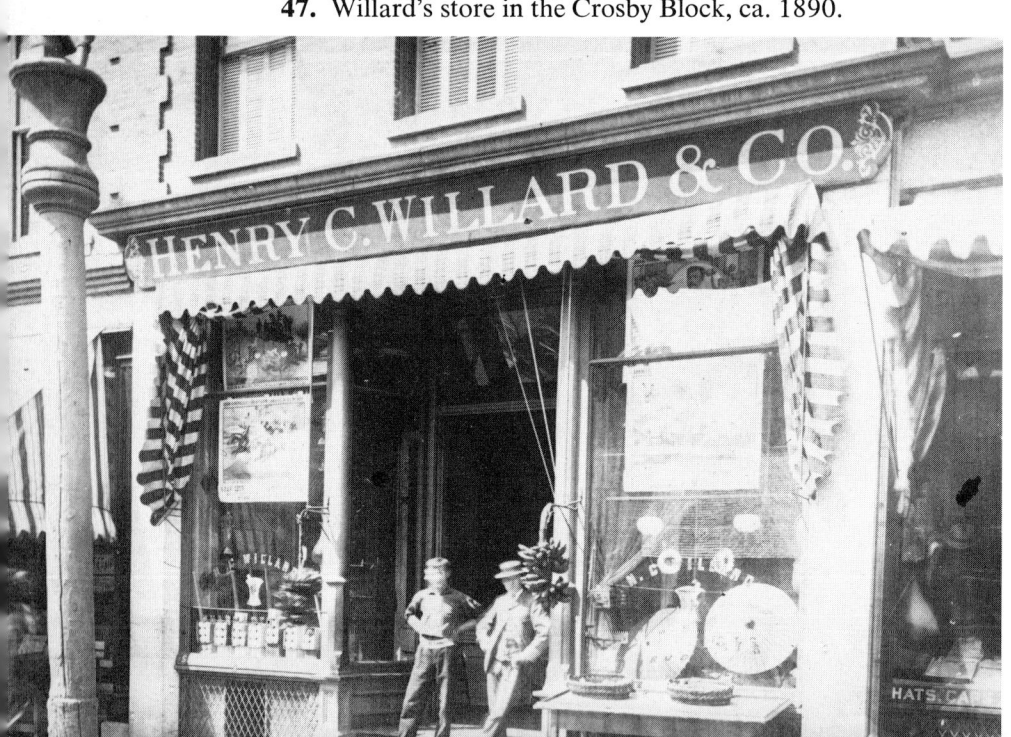

The block of Main Street leveled by the 1869 fire was entirely occupied, when rebuilt, by two structures: the Brooks House and the Crosby Block (**45**). As the picture shows, the Crosby Block was nearly completed when the Brooks House was still a vacant lot. When the two buildings were finished, this part of Main Street had acquired the essentials of its present-day appearance. Most of the ground floor of the Crosby Block was taken by retail merchants—note the bunches of bananas outside Willard's (**47**). The Elliot Street corner, however, was leased by the Vermont National Bank (their sign is visible in **49**); these are the same premises the Bank occupies today.

Edward Crosby, who built the Crosby Block, was born in West Brattleboro. He was a partner in several flour mill businesses before he established E. Crosby & Co. In 1887 he built a new mill east of the railroad tracks (**48**). The photograph, taken sometime during the years when modern-style freight cars and horse-drawn carts were contemporaries, shows the cellar hole and foundations of the old flour mill (**34**) west of the tracks.

49. Elliot Street from Main, 1870's.

Well into the 1870's, Brattleboro's fire protection came from small volunteer fire companies scattered around town. Membership in a fire company was a mark of considerable social standing; a good part of the volunteers' efforts went into parades, drills, and competitions with rival companies. A full-dress parade in Brattleboro might have included men and equipment from Hydropath Engine Company, Fountain Engine Company, Phoenix Engine Company, and Protector Hook and Ladder Company. Bands played and the men marched in red, white and blue uniforms.

50. The officers of Fountain Company No. 4, 1870.

51. Old firehouse, Church and Elliot streets, 1905.

52. Central Fire Station, Elliot Street, early 1900's.

53. West Brattleboro hand pumper, vintage 1865.

A Central Fire Station was built in 1873 on the north side of Elliot Street, just east of what is now the driveway to the Harmony Place parking lot. The portrait (**52**) from the early years of this century shows the horse-drawn equipment in use at that time. In the background, on top of the Grange Block, is the roof garden of the Vermont Wheel Club, a fashionable bicycling association.

Jubilee Jim Fisk—The Robber Baron Who Was Martyred for Love

54. Col. James Fisk, Jr.

55. Miss Josie Mansfield.

Col. James Fisk, Jr. pursued for a brief thirty-seven years the most brilliant and notorious career of any citizen of Brattleboro. Born in 1835 in Pownal, he moved with his family to Brattleboro as a small boy. His father, James Fisk, Sr., was an itinerant pedlar turned respectable citizen who built the Revere House in 1849 and opened it as a temperance hotel. Young Jim, who had by this time spent three years with a traveling circus, did return to help his father, but the confines of Brattleboro were too narrow to hold him long.

Fisk's first adventures in finance were made possible by the Civil War. He speculated in blockaded southern cotton, and in the sale of worthless Confederate bonds in England. After the war, Fisk went into business on Wall Street with Daniel Drew and Jay Gould. The three masterminded the long and victorious battle with "Commodore" Vanderbilt for control of the Erie Railroad; having won, they milked the decrepit line for millions. Fisk's greatest exploit, again in partnership with Gould, was an attempt to obtain a corner in the gold market. The plan very nearly succeeded, ruining enough investors to produce the "Black Friday" panic of September 24, 1869.

Fisk's popular appeal lay in his combination of roughshod financial wizardry with an insatiable appetite for the finer things. "Jubilee Jim" was renowned for his diamonds, his capacity for champagne and oysters, his impulsive purchase of an opera house. It was, of course, a woman that got

56. The Fisk monument, Prospect Hill Cemetery.

57. Revere House, corner of Main and Elliot Streets, 1872.

him into trouble. The great love of his life, Josie Mansfield, had been giving more than encouragement to a one-time Fisk associate named Ed Stokes. On January 7, 1872, in one of the most sensational murders of the century, Stokes shot and killed Fisk on the staircase of the Broadway Central Hotel, New York City. Jubilee Jim's massive remains were shipped to Brattleboro and lay in state at the Revere House. The entire town turned out for the funeral at the Baptist Church on Main Street and followed the cortège to Prospect Hill Cemetery. Larkin G. Mead, the local sculptor who had created the "Snow Angel," was commissioned to create a suitable memorial. Mead responded by producing another typical work. Four vaguely clad female figures adorn the Fisk monument: one bears a sheaf of railway shares; another, steamship holdings; a third, a sack of coins; the last, an emblem of Fisk's patronage of the stage.

Jim Fisk, Sr., lived out his days at the Retreat, a pillar of respectability.

58. Menu for the Odd Fellows banquet, 1869.

Wantastiquet Lodge
No. 5, I. O. O. F.

REVERE HOUSE,
Monday Eve'g, April 26, 1869.

SUPPER BILL OF FARE.

OYSTERS—STEWED.

BOILED.
CHICKEN, CURRANT JELLY, CORNED BEEF, ROLLED AND PRESSED,
BEEF TONGUE, PICKLED LAMBS TONGUE,
SUGAR CURED HAMS, GARNISHED.

ROAST.
BEEF, TURKEY, PORK, CHICKEN, LAMB.

BAKED.
CHICKEN PIES. ESCALOPED OYSTERS, HAM.

FRIED.
PICKLED PIGS FEET, OYSTERS,
OYSTER FRITTERS, TRIPE.

SALADS.
LOBSTER SALAD, CHICKEN SALAD.

LOBSTERS.

RELISHES.
PICKLED CUCUMBERS, WORCESTERSHIRE SAUCE,
LETTUCE, COLD SLAW, RADISHES,
TOMATO CATSUP,
HORSE RADISH, PICKLED BEETS, MIXED PICKLES, CUCUMBERS, CHEESE.

BREAD.
WHEAT BREAD, BOSTON BROWN BREAD,
FRENCH ROLLS, SODA BISCUIT.

PASTRY.
MEAT PIE, APPLE PIE, SQUASH PIE,
PEACH PIE, BLACKBERRY PIE, LEMON PIE,
COCOANUT PIE. WASHINGTON CREAM PIE.

CAKE.
FRUIT CAKE, WHITE MOUNTAIN CAKE, POUND CAKE, RAISIN CAKE,
CHOCOLATE CAKE, CITRON CAKE, GOLD CAKE, ORANGE CAKE,
CURRANT CAKE, CUP CAKE, JELLY CAKE, COCOANUT CAKE,
SILVER CAKE, SPONGE CAKE,
JELLY IN PASTE, LADY FINGERS, COCOANUT DROPS. KISSES.

SWEETMEATS AND JELLIES.
CANNED STRAWBERRY, CANNED PEACH, CANNED QUINCE,
BLACKBERRY, HONEY, PORT WINE JELLY,
LEMON JELLY, JELLY WITH FRUIT, STRAWBERRY JELLY,
RASPBERRY JELLY, SHERRY WINE JELLY.

CREAMS.
LEMON, VANILLA, RASPBERRY, ORANGE,
VELVET, CHOCOLATE, STRAWBERRY, COCOANUT.
CHARLOTTE RUSSE IN MOULDS.

FRUIT.
ORANGES, APPLES, FILBERTS, ALMONDS,
ENGLISH WALNUTS, HICKORY NUTS, PECAN NUTS, CASTANA NUTS,
LAYER RAISINS, SHREDED PINE APPLE.

VANILLA ICE CREAM, STRAWBERRY ICE CREAM.

TEA, CHOCOLATE, COFFEE.

G. A. BOYDEN, Proprietor.

59. Revere House fire, 1877.

James Fisk, Sr., opened the Revere House in 1849. It passed through several hands thereafter and was periodically renovated. The body of Col. James Fisk, Jr., was displayed in Room No. 1 before his Brattleboro funeral in 1872. In 1877 a fire broke out in the Revere House stables, a short distance west on Elliot Street. It spread toward Main Street, and destroyed the hotel. The stone Dickinson Building (visible to the left in **57**) was damaged but later rebuilt.

VICTORIAN HEYDAY

J. Estey & Co., manufacturers of parlor or "cottage" organs, was the most important commercial enterprise in the history of Brattleboro. Jacob Estey himself did not start the business, but in the best entrepreneurial tradition of the nineteenth century he built and guided it, creating a great popular institution as he did so. Estey organs from Brattleboro were carried as far as Australia and New Zealand.

60. First Estey shop, Canal Street, ca. 1856.
61. Second Estey shop (left foreground), Plaza Park site, ca. 1860.

Estey's first workshop (**60**) faced southeast onto Canal Street, near the Main Street Bridge. His first undertaking in Brattleboro was the pipe and pump business on the right in the picture. Estey also dealt in gravestones, some of which appear to be leaning on the front porch—the location was convenient to Prospect Hill Cemetery. By the time of the photograph Estey had bought into the fledgling organ business. This operation was carried on under the name of Estey & Green from 1855 until 1865, when it was reorganized as J. Estey & Co. When the first building burned down in 1857, Estey built a new shop for his businesses across the street on the future site of Plaza Park (**61**). The building to the right in the picture, advertising "Furniture," was erected on the site of the burned out shop: Estey did not work there himself but rented out the space. (Note the cemetery on top of the hill at the left.)

62. Officers of J. Estey & Co.

63.

Estey sold his gravestone business in 1858 and his pipe and pump business in 1864, and from then on concentrated in parlor organs. In 1866 he took his son and son-in-law into the business; this partnership guided the Estey fortunes through the firm's great years. In the portrait (**62**), from left to right, are Julius J. Estey, Levi K. Fuller, and Jacob Estey. They are posed with the firm's model *de luxe,* also featured in the advertising poster (**63**).

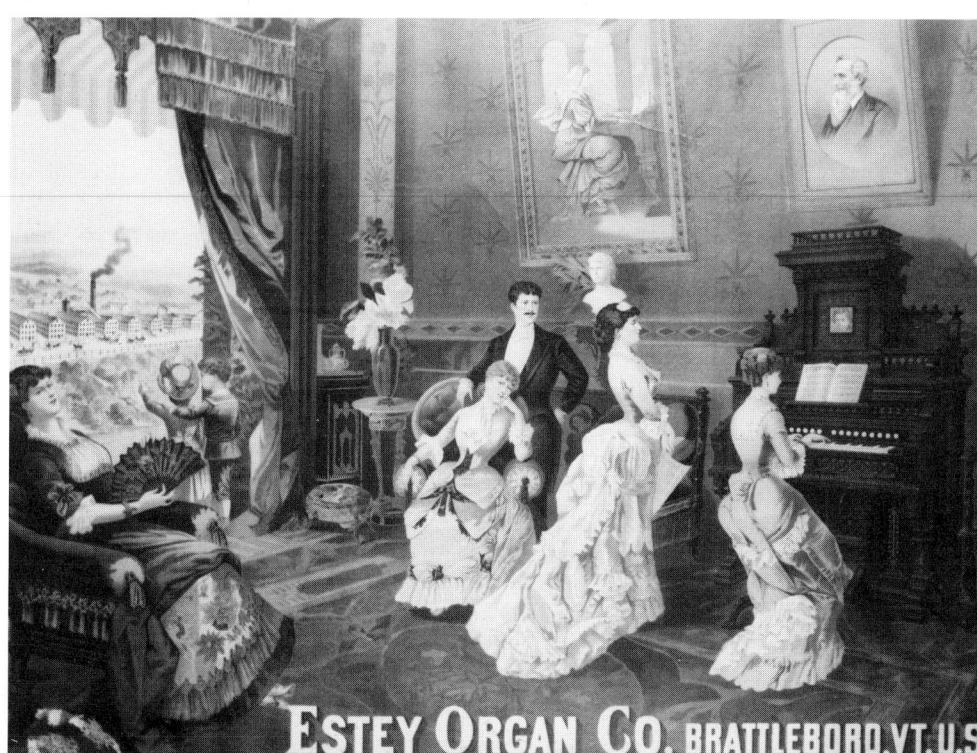

64.

> Office of the
> ESTEY ORGAN COMPANY.
> Brattleboro Vt.
>
> April 12, 1886.
>
> TO WHOM IT MAY CONCERN:
>
> We are informed that reports are in circulation by unreliable parties, to the effect that Mr. Jacob Estey, the founder of the Estey Organ Company, is dead, and that no genuine Estey Organs are in the market at the present time.
>
> We wish to deny these statements wholly, and to say that Mr. Estey, Senior, is in good health, and attends to business six days in the week.
>
> We are turning out a very large number of Estey Organs each month, doubtless more than double the production of any other factory in the world.
>
> Of course, with so flattering a business we are blessed with a small army of imitators, and their methods are varied and in some instances unscrupulous.
>
> The Estey Organ, however, still retains, and we expect always will retain, its supremacy over all competitors.
>
> Very truly,
>
> Estey Organ Company.
>
> Dictated by *Jacob Estey*

Increasing business lead the Esteys to construct, in 1866, a large factory at Frost and Elm streets. After most of its lumber stock was lost in the flood of 1869, the company bought sixty acres on Birge Street and erected the sprawling organ works featured in later advertisements. Eight factory buildings fronted on Birge Street, each three stories high and a hundred feet long; there was also a storehouse, an engine house, a wood-drying house, a blacksmith shop and a firehouse. The business prospered. In some weeks four carloads of black walnut lumber for organ cases would be shipped to Brattleboro. When the end-of-day whistle blew, the sidewalks were thronged with homebound "operatives." Most of the buildings remain today as a memorial to Brattleboro's industrial past.

65. A trade card of 1897.

66. Estey Works, Birge Street, ca. 1880.

67. Estate of Julius Estey, Florence Terrace off School Street.

The Estey family's name is associated with noteworthy Brattleboro buildings other than the family's organ factories. The home shown above (**67**) was built in 1853 for John Stoddard, later acquired by Julius Estey, Jacob's son. In 1971 its shell was torn down to make room for a housing development. The home of J. Harry Estey (son of Julius), on Putney Road, was sold in 1929 to become the Elks' Home.

68. Home of J. Harry Estey, Putney Road.

The early workshop scene could well have been at the Frost Street factory, which appears to be represented in the medallion on the painted wagon (**71**). The proud display of the world's largest organ reed pipe took place on Washington Street, about 1921 (**70**).

69. Estey shop interior, ca. 1870.

70.

71.

Railroads

72. Railroad yards from Prospect Hill, 1870's.
73. Mouth of Whetstone Brook, ca. 1880.

74.

The railroad came to Brattleboro on February 20, 1849. On that day the Vermont & Massachusetts Rail Road, built north from Millers Falls, ran its first train into town. Sixteen cars carrying 1500 passengers arrived at the depot "amid cheers and shouts of the multitude."

Brattleboro has had three railroad stations. The first station, built in 1849, is visible in the view from Prospect Hill (**72**). The depot is just in front of the gasworks' smokestack near the covered bridge. This building was replaced by an ornate brick station in 1881, which in turn gave way to the present station in 1915.

The first bridge of the Vermont Valley road over Whetstone Brook was the covered bridge seen in **34**. This wooden structure caught fire frequently from the sparks of the locomotives; it was replaced in 1878 by a handsome stone arch (**73**). The arch stands today, but it is hidden between a wooden walkway and a modern steel bridge. Since the completion of the Vernon Dam in 1911 the water beneath the arch has been much higher than it appears in the picture.

Three dapper conductors (**74**) from the Vt. and Mass. RR are, left to right, J. N. O'Hare, H. D. Carroll, and Jake Bangs.

August of 1886 saw two of Brattleboro's greatest train wrecks. The most famous was the collapse of the West River bridge on the narrow gauge West River Railroad (**76**). On the afternoon of Wednesday, August 18, a ten car train was pulling across the river into town when the bridge collapsed, suddenly and completely. Two people were killed in the disaster, which was never satisfactorily explained. A new steel bridge was eventually constructed; to reassure the public, it was tested with ten flat cars each carrying twenty tons of Dummerston granite. Twelve days earlier, the northbound *White Mountain Express* derailed just south of Brattleboro station (**75**). The cause of the wreck was a flatcar (in the foreground) which rolled from a spur and blocked the main line. This time no one was killed.

75. Wreck of the *White Mountain Express,* August 6, 1886.

76. Collapse of West River bridge, August 18, 1886.

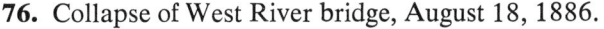

77. Last narrow gauge West River train, 1905.

78. Station baggage room, 1901.

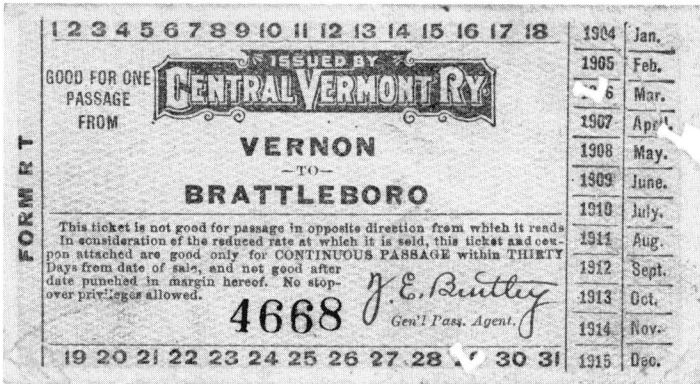

79.

80. Brattleboro's second station, 1880's.

From 1881 to 1915 Brattleboro's railroad station was an ornate brick structure on the present site of the Merrill Gas Company. Until 1905, some of its tracks provided a third rail to accommodate the narrow-gauge equipment of the West River trains. Notice (in **77**) the wood burning locomotive, its smokestack fitted with a screen to catch flying embers. The baggage room wall bears a black bordered portrait of William McKinley, killed by an assassin's bullet in 1901. The construction gang of Irish "railway navvies" (**81**) posed for a portrait on the Boston & Maine railway bridge south of Brattleboro.

81. Irish construction gang, early 1900's.

The Retreat

In 1834 Mrs. Anna Marsh, the widow of Dr. Perley Marsh of Hinsdale, N.H. (**82**), left a bequest of $10,000 for the establishment of a mental hospital in Windham County, Vermont, near the Connecticut River. The site eventually chosen was the estate of Nathan Woodcock, just north of Brattleboro, on the west side of Dummerston Road. Here were six acres of ground and a house (**83**) large enough to accommodate twenty patients. The new hospital, known at first as the Vermont Lunatic Asylum, opened its doors on November 30, 1836. This was the origin of the famous Brattleboro Retreat, one of the first hospitals in the country designed for the scientific treatment of mental illness.

The Retreat grew rapidly. As early as 1838 the hospital expanded, erecting a new building east of Dummerston Road—the first building on what are today the main grounds of the Retreat. With subsequent additions, this became the Old Main building, still standing. The original Woodcock house, on the west side of the road, was replaced in 1857 by the Marsh Building; this was incorporated in 1939 into the long, three-story building known today as Linden Lodge Nursing Home. The familiar Retreat Farm (**86**), on the site of the Arms Tavern, was purchased in 1858. The Retreat continued to grow, and in the twentieth century saw the addition of such buildings as Lawton Hall (**85**), originally known as the Casino.

A Brattleboro curiosity, the battlemented stone tower on Chestnut Hill, (**88**) was constructed by the Retreat to add glamour to the elaborate system of woodland paths it had laid out in that area for the recreation of its patients. Built in 1887, the tower is today a reminder of the fashion for architectural extravagances that was a feature of the period.

82. Marsh House, Hinsdale, N.H.

83. First Retreat Building, ca. 1850.

84. Country Club, Upper Dummerston Road, originally the Retreat Men's Summer cottage.

85. Lawton Hall, "The Casino."

86. Retreat Farm, Dummerston Road.

87. Old Main Building.

88. Tower.

Shows...

Sports...

Service...

89. Barnum and Bailey advertising booklet, 1896.

90. Circus parade, 1898.

91. High School football team, 1898.

Barnum and Bailey's Circus, the greatest show on earth, as advertised, came to Brattleboro on July 10, 1896. The attractions of the performance were advertised well in advance. Admission was fifty cents with reserved seats available at Geo. Greene's Drug Store, on Main Street. The full Circus staged a spectacular street parade on the morning of the show.

The parades of smaller circuses in other years were less imposing but fun just the same. The baby elephant (**90**) marching south past the Brooks House belonged to Walter Main's Circus, which came to town in September, 1898.

Another diversion of 1898 was the Brattleboro High School football team

(91), state champions that year. Brattleboro's first post office was established in 1784, probably in the Arms Tavern on the site of the Retreat Farm. Its location changed frequently until 1917, when the Post Office was given its own building at Main and Grove Streets. From 1862 until 1917, the Post Office had its headquarters in various parts of the old Town Hall. It was there that the staff posed for a portrait (92) in about 1900. It is interesting to note that the carriers' uniforms had by this time been modeled on Spanish-American War uniforms, whereas ten years earlier (93) they still resembled the uniforms of the Civil War.

92. Post Office in the Town Hall, ca. 1900.

93. Mailmen, ca. 1890.

94. Mail was delivered on Washington St. in spite of the Blizzard of '88.

95. The old High School, Main Street, 1869.

96. Esteyville School, top of Estey Hill, 1899.

Scholars...

Soldiers...

The central part of Brattleboro's first high school was built in 1832. North and south wings were added in 1868. The building (**95**) stood on the present site of the Municipal Building—the lamp post in the picture is at the point between Main and Linden Streets. The old school was replaced in 1884 by a new brick school, which eventually became the Municipal Building.

In 1874 Julius Estey organized the Estey Guard, and made himself Captain. This was a kind of national guard regiment whose main function was drilling and parading, although the Guard did enlist for service in the Spanish-American War. As a parade group the Guard was much in demand, appearing all over New England and as far away as Washington. In the photograph at right (**97**) they are marching down Main Street past the old Town Hall. At the corner of High Street is an interesting three-way drinking fountain: one trough for men, one for horses, and one for dogs. In the background, east of Main Street, is the Clapp House.

97. Main Street parade, ca. 1880.

98. The Estey Guard, 1870's.

99. Miss Mary Howe, 1888.

Although, like many another prima donna, Mary Howe concealed her birthdate, she was born in Brattleboro in the mid-1860's. She was the daughter of C. L. Howe, farmer turned pioneer photographer, who operated a successful portrait studio in the Union Block on Main Street. Mary Howe studied singing in Boston and Philadelphia, then sailed for Europe and made a brilliant debut singing *La Sonnambula* in Berlin. She later sang in Wiesbaden by invitation of Kaiser Wilhelm. She made her American debut in Brattleboro in August 1888, then returned to Europe where she continued to perform until 1905.

Kipling in Vermont

When Rudyard Kipling, who had married an American girl, moved to the Brattleboro area in 1892, he was already famous though only twenty-six. Among Kipling's best known works, *The Jungle Books,* were produced during his four years residence in Brattleboro and just over the town line in Dummerston. Kipling and his wife (Caroline Balestier) spent their first winter in Brattleboro in the Bliss Cottage on the northern end of town. They then moved into "Naulakha," the house built for them in Dummerston. Kipling worked hard and productively here. Reporters from the city papers came up by train and journeyed to Naulakha by carriage or sleigh, but generally left without an interview. Kipling's objection to being

101. Kipling doodle, 1892.

102. Kipling "regrets."

100. Kipling on Main Street, 1893.

103. Kipling's Dummerston home, "Naulakha," as it looked around the turn of the century.

photographed was even more pronounced. A surreptitious shot of the author (**100**) standing in front of the Baptist Church is one of the few pictures of him in Brattleboro. Withdrawn from the public as Kipling was, his friends and neighbors in Brattleboro described him as a warm and hospitable companion. The author interested himself in Brattleboro affairs. Entering the debate over whether or not to build a trolley line in town, Kipling declared he was very much against a course that would destroy "the beauty for which Brattleboro is so justly famous."

The author evidently enjoyed life at Naulakha, and he might have contemplated a much longer stay but for a bitter falling-out with his brother-in-law, who was his neighbor in Dummerston. The incident became scandal for the metropolitan newspapers, and the pleasure Kipling had taken in his Vermont estate was soured. He and his wife, with their two Vermont-born daughters, sailed for England in September 1896.

104. Glenwood Ladies' Seminary, West Brattleboro, 1860's.
105. Glenwood ladies of the Class of 1869.

West Brattleboro

The Glenwood Ladies' Seminary, established in 1860, occupied the buildings of the earlier Brattleborough Academy in West Brattleboro. The Seminary was only one of a series of educational institutions that succeeded each other in these buildings, with considerable turnover in schoolmasters. In 1881, while looking for a new man to take over, the weary trustees specified that the candidate "must have the power to a reasonable degree of drawing in pupils, instructing, and retaining them." The central building of the three (**104**) survived the longest, known for many years as the West Brattleboro Academy. It was torn down in the 1950's and the new West Brattleboro School was built to the east of its site.

106. West Brattleboro, looking west on Western Avenue, 1890's.

Two views of West Brattleboro in the 1890's present an appearance that is very familiar today. The old bandstand (**107**) stood in front of South Street, which goes up the hill to the left. The present West Brattleboro fire station is now located on a site in the left foreground of this scene.

107. West Brattleboro Common, ca. 1895.

108. Western Avenue, looking west toward Whetstone Brook, ca. 1890.

109. "Aunt Sally" Stockwell, aged 103.

110. Aunt Sally's 100th birthday party.

111. Marsh's Brickyard, Ames Hill, 1893.

The bridge across Whetstone Brook on Western Avenue (**108**) is traditionally the eastern limit of West Brattleboro. Most of the houses in this picture remain today; the covered bridge was replaced by a concrete bridge in 1908. The old wooden bridge was notable as one that did *not* get swept away in the 1869 flood.

One of West Brattleboro's most famous residents was "Aunt Sally" Stockwell, for many years the oldest inhabitant of the State of Vermont. Born Sally Harris on April 30, 1779 in Chesterfield, N.H., she moved with her family to Ames Hill as a small girl. At the age of sixteen she married Arad Stockwell; in 1837 they retired from Ames Hill to Greenleaf Street in West Brattleboro, where Aunt Sally lived until her death September 21, 1883. The portrait photograph was taken for a stereoscopic slide when she was 103. The other picture shows the celebration on Greenleaf Street for Aunt Sally's 100th birthday.

Marsh's Brickyard (**111**) was at the corner of Ames Hill Road and Covey Road. Note the rows of bricks drying in the sun and the woodpile, used for firing the brick.

112. Clark Tavern, lower Canal Street.

113. Joseph Goodhue House, Main Street.

114. Brooks Library.

Buildings of Note ... A brief tour

115. Cune/Thompson houses, Main Street.

The Rufus Clark Tavern (**112**) was built in 1812; the site on Canal Street is now occupied by The Montgomery Ward Auto Service Center. The houses of the Cune and Thompson families (**115**) stood side-by-side on the site of the present Post Office building. Brattleboro's free public library was established in 1882 in rooms in the Town Hall. Its first real home was built in 1886 (**114**), by George Brooks (the builder of the Brooks House) on the Main Street site previously occupied by the Joseph Goodhue homestead (**113**). The colonnaded house at the corner of Elliot and Elm Streets (**116**) is still standing, but its facade has been converted to a storefront and is scarcely recognizable. "Reed's Castle" (**118**) was an early apartment house on Green Street at the top of Church Street. The superb Deacon John Holbrook House (**117**), still standing at the corner of Chapin and Linden Streets, was built about 1825 by Captain Nathaniel Bliss for the Holbrooks. For another son, Rev. John Calvin Holbrook, Deacon Holbrook built the magnificent brick house (**119**) on Main Street at the corner of Harris Place. This house was torn down in 1940. It had fourteen rooms and five fireplaces; the gardens ran the length of Harris Place to overlook the Connecticut River.

116. Lovell Farr House, Elliot and Elm Streets.

117. Deacon John Holbrook House, Chapin and Linden Streets.

118. "Reed's Castle," Green Street, ca. 1880.

119. Rev. Dr. John Calvin Holbrook House, Main Street.

120. Congregational Church, West Brattleboro, 1880's.

The First Congregational Church in West Brattleboro (**120**) was built in 1845, replacing an earlier church that had burned; this is the same building that stands today, though its appearance has been considerably altered. West Brattleboro's most famous octagon

121. Octagon House, West Brattleboro, 1890's.

house (**121**) stood across the street from the same church on Western Avenue. There was a brief vogue for these handsome houses in the mid-nineteenth century. The virtue of the octagon house, on one theory, was that in it the builder came as close as was practicable to achieving a house in the figure of a circle, supposedly the most perfect form in nature. The Universalist Church (**122**) was built in 1851 near the corner of Clark and Canal Streets. In 1933 the steeple was removed, and the church became the Grange Hall. The C. E. Allen House (**123**) still stands at 192 Canal Street. At the time of the photograph, Allen was running a thriving flower and seed business: his hothouses covered an area of half an acre. The pleasant view of Walnut Street in the 1890's (**124**) shows Mrs. Kirkland's boarding house on the left; this is the present site of the Fleming Oil Company. The Francis Goodhue house (**125**) stood on the east side of Main Street until 1922, when it was demolished to make room for the Community Building. The Dowley Place (**126**) still stands on Main Street, across from the library; but the house is hidden behind a set of shops and the lawn has become a filling station. The view north on Main Street (**127**) gives a good idea of Brattleboro in its prettiest days. To the right are the old Town Hall, the Clapp house, and the Congregational Church; to the left are the Hunt house and the Baptist Church. The Hunt house stood until 1929, when it was replaced by the Montgomery Ward store on Main Street. The inset (**129**) shows the central staircase of the Hunt house. House built for Frederick Zelotes Dickinson (**128**) on the site of former Bliss Farm in the early 1900's, afterwards belonged to Dorothy Bibby, later Dorothy Persons, the daughter of Mayor Gilroy of New York City. On her death in 1962, "Sandanona," as it came to be called, was sold to the Experiment in International Living.

122. Universalist Church.

123. Allen House.

124. Walnut Street, looking east.

125. Francis Goodhue house, Main Street.

126. The Dowley Place, Main Street.

127. Looking north from High and Main Streets, 1890's.

128. F. Z. Dickinson residence, later named "Sandanona."

129.

REFORMER EXTRA!

BRATTLEBORO, VT., JUNE 16, 1880.

Bank Smash!

THE FIRST NATIONAL BANK OF BRATTLEBORO RUINED,

BY THE DEFALCATION OF COL SILAS. M. WAITE, ITS PRESIDENT, WHO HAS RUN AWAY.

THE LOSS VARIOUSLY ESTIMATED AT FROM

$100,000 TO $500,000.

FORGERY AND WHAT OTHER CRIMES.

A BIG CRACK IN THE UPPER CRUST.

Ruin and Woe for Many People

The most startling crime which ever broke upon this county, and possibly as it the bank. A few moments' examination satisfied them that something was wrong, and the deeper they probed, the blacker things looked. They found a note bearing the signature of C. J. Amidon, which that gentleman himself immediately declared a forgery. The signature of the late C. C. Waite, of New York, on considerable other paper was likewise pronounced a forgery. It was also found that a large number of notes which have been shown to the directors at the late "investigations" as among the assets of the bank, are missing, and the supposition is that they were forgeries and that Waite destroyed them before clearing out. The directors, after investigating long enough yesterday, to be satisfied that their institution was ruined, took an adjournment to 10 o'clock to-day, when they will probably settle upon some further plans of action.

Meanwhile a suit was brought against Waite late yesterday afternoon, in behalf of the bank, claiming $200,000 and attaching every scrap of visible property is that he has gone off and committed suicide. But this is merely a supposition with no evidence whatever to support it, so far as we know. Still another theory is held by a few who retain their faith in Waite's fertility of resources, and believe that he only left to raise money in some way to ease up present difficulties, and will yet return and face the music with his old-time grit.

As to the extent of the loss, nothing more than the merest guessing in the dark can yet be done. There is some paper against home parties that is good, if it does not prove to be forged like that against Amidon. But the great bulk of the notes are against parties in the west, or in distant cities, and from what is already known it is naturally expected that this will mainly prove to be forged. In fact the investigation so far as it has proceeded, indicates that the institution has been kept afloat by forgeries and false entries for some time. But there is no evidence yet that Col. Waite has got any forged paper discounted at any other banks. One director said last stitution. He was a poor man when appointed cashier but very soon became prominent in various business enterprises. He has been largely interested in the manufacture of carriages, of cottage organs, here and at Chicago; he owns all the stock of the Brattleboro Gas Company, the Hinsdale stock company, and is an extensive owner of real estate. He has been prominent in railroad circles as a director in the Vermont Valley, Connecticut River, and formerly of the West River railroad. One enterprise he was pushing up to the day he left town was the proposed railroad from Brattleboro to Hinsdale. From about 1862 to 1867 he controlled both the politics and the business of Brattleboro. He represented the town in the legislature and came near being nominated by a Republican State convention for State treasurer. He took upon himself the management of town, village and school district matters. He has ceased of late to run the town and village but has had everything his own way in the management of the affairs of the school district. Unlike most defaulters in modern

130. June 16, 1880.

131. A local three dollar bill, ca. 1860.

GOOD TIMES

One of Brattleboro's greatest scandals, out of place in this generally tranquil era, was the failure of the First National Bank in June 1880, caused by the "defalcation" of its President, Silas M. Waite. From humble beginnings in Newfane, Waite had become a leading power in the business and politics of Brattleboro. According to the *Reformer,* Waite's "peculiar, magnetic composition enabled him to exercise almost unlimited power over those he permitted to be on his board of directors." After the bank failed, the *Reformer* indulged itself in saying "I told you so," especially to its rival, *The Vermont Phoenix,* which had evidently been printing reassuring stories on the Bank's condition.

The Wheel Club

The Vermont Wheel Club, successor in 1885 to the Brattleboro Bicycle Club, was the leading social organization of the town in an era when club life had its greatest influence. The Wheel Club was a center of every kind of sporting and social activity in Brattleboro. Club projects included balls and banquets, baseball games and clambakes, parades and field days—as well as bicycle races. From 1895 to 1914 the Wheel Club was located in the Grange Block on the north side of Elliot Street. This building burned in January, 1914 (**134**); the next year a new building was erected on the same site, and the Club installed new facilities there. In 1924, the Wheel Club became the Brattleboro Club.

132. H. L. Emerson, Wheel Club President, 1885.

133. Vermont Wheel Club emblem.

134. Grange Block fire, Jan. 18, 1914, Elliot St.

135. "Lindenhurst," top of Green Street, before alterations.

136. G. E. Crowell.

George Crowell came to Brattleboro from Massachusetts in 1866 to publish "The Household," a highly successful women's weekly paper with offices in the Crosby Block. In 1886 Crowell purchased the Buckner house at the top of Green Street, renamed it "Lindenhurst," and started extensive alterations. The renovated mansion had thirty-seven rooms and was decorated throughout with elaborate woodwork—as many as twelve kinds of wood were used in a single room. "Lindenhurst" was razed in 1936; lot is today a playground near the junction of High and Green Streets.

In 1882 Crowell had bought Hines Hill, which he renamed Chestnut Hill; he completed a reservoir and aqueduct begun by former owner Isaac Hines and opened "Highland Park" to the people of Brattleboro. Walks, drives, and seats were provided (including a summer house, **137**). The most notable structure was a "Swiss cottage" next to the reservoir (**138**), where invalids, orphans, and Fresh Air Fund children were sent for summer vacations.

137. "The Bird's Nest," Highland Park, Chestnut Hill.

138. Chestnut Hill Reservoir and Crowell Cottage.

139. Levi Fuller, ca. 1859.

140. Fuller house, "Pine Heights," 1880's.

141. Governor Fuller and wife at "Pine Heights," ca. 1890.

142. Timothy Vinton.

143. Vinton's Paper Mill, from South Main Street.

Levi K. Fuller was born in Westmoreland, N.H. in 1841 and came to Brattleboro at the age of thirteen to work as a printer's apprentice. While still in his teens he became known as an inventor and mechanic: the drawing (**139**) shows him with a steam engine he built which won a prize at the Windham County Fair. Fuller went to work for Jacob Estey in 1860. In 1865 he married Abby Estey, the boss's daughter, and in 1866 he was made a vice-president of the firm. Fuller made several important contributions to the techniques of reed organ construction, and by the end of his life he had over a hundred patented inventions. He served as Governor of Vermont from 1892 to 1894. Fuller and his wife lived in "Pine Heights" (**140**), which he built on Canal Street in 1876. The Governor had installed a large telescope with which to further his study of astronomy. The site is now occupied by the Eden Park Nursing Home.

Vinton's Paper Mill (**143**), successor to the first paper mill in Brattleboro, stood on the south side of Whetstone Brook, across from South Main Street. The site is now occupied by the Plaza Shopping Center parking lot. Timothy Vinton (**142**) ran the mill from 1847 until his death in 1890. From then until 1930 the mill was run, successively, by three more generations of Vintons.

An Honest Dollar

The load being pulled up Main Street by fourteen horses was the new steel doors for the vault at People's National Bank.

144. A fourteen-horse hitch, Main Street, ca. 1900.

145. Bond's hearse, Van Doorn Building.

William H. Bond's Undertaking Parlors occupied the ground floor of the Van Doorn Building, on the east side of Main Street across from Flat Street.

146. William H. Bond's Undertaking Parlors, ca. 1900.

147. Scott & Jones Grocery Store, Main Street, 1890's.

148. Clapp & Jones Bookstore, Main Street, 1894.

The interior views of retail stores on Main Street give an idea of shopping in downtown Brattleboro in the 1890's. The Union Block (**149**)—here decorated with flags for the Valley Fair—contained typical storefronts. One method of advertisement adopted by local merchants was to distribute small trade cards bearing amusing drawings and printed with the name of the store (**150–152**). These came in series and could be collected, as baseball cards are today.

149. Union Block, Main Street, 1890's.

150.

151.

152.

153. Inspecting overalls.

154. C. H. Eddy salesman, and companion, ca. 1893.

Overalls were manufactured at the Hooker, Corser, and Mitchell plant on Frost Street. The lady to the right (**153**) is Mrs. Minnie Bliss, forelady for forty years. A traveling salesman is shown in his delivery wagon in front of C. H. Eddy's Flat Street bottling works. This business was a forerunner of today's DeWitt Beverage Company.

Built in 1866, the factory buildings at Elm and Frost Streets (**156**) housed Estey's organ works until the flood of 1869. After the flood, Jacob Estey decided to relocate his factories on higher ground. The Brattleboro Manufacturing Company, makers of wooden furniture, held the Elm and Frost Streets factories from 1869 to 1880, when Smith & Hunt moved in. Fire destroyed the buildings in 1899.

Smith & Hunt made baby carriages. Two of their products are seen in operation (**155**) on an autumn day in 1906. The occupants of the carriages are Howard Rice, Jr. (left) and Lyman Adams, attended by their mothers.

155. Out for a stroll, Fall 1906.

156. Smith & Hunt factory, Elm and Frost Streets.

157. Steam Laundry, Flat Street, early 1900's.

158. Delivering logs, Frost Street, ca. 1910.

159. Main Street horse auction, ca. 1880.

The scene at the corner of Main and Elliot (**159**) is apparently a horse auction—fine thoroughbreds were sometimes auctioned in Brattleboro. The load of logs (**158**) is being delivered to a local sawmill. Note the curved saplings above the load, used to keep taut the chains that hold the logs. The Steam Laundry on Flat Street (**157**) occupied the present site of the Latchis Hotel parking lot.

160. J. A. Church boiler explosion, Frost Street, 1886.

161.

The J. A. Church woodworking and gristmill was on the Frost Street site later occupied by Holden and Martin's woodworking shop. In 1886 the factory boiler exploded. The boiler demolished the engine house at the mill (**160**), flew over a two-story building and landed 260 feet away. It then rebounded and crashed through the side of a barn (**161**) killing a horse that was tethered outside.

162. Auditorium, interior.

The old Town Hall, on the east side of Main Street at High, was built in 1855. It contained the Post Office and several small businesses and meeting rooms, as well as the town offices. The largest room was the "Festival Hall," which held conventions, concerts, and lectures by such speakers as Mark Twain, Oliver Wendell Holmes, Henry Ward Beecher, and Horace Greeley.

In 1895 the citizens of Brattleboro voted to expand the Town Hall. A signal addition was the Opera House, or Auditorium. This was an elegant 900-seat theater modeled after the old Abbey Theater in New York. It was decorated with hand-cast plaster moldings, brass fittings, and a painted curtain. The excellent facilities attracted many stage companies: among the greatest successes were appearances by Will Rogers, John Philip Sousa, and Alfred Lunt. The increasing popularity of movies marked the end of the Auditorium's golden years, though the stage remained for occasional use. The Town Hall with its theater was torn down in 1953; the site is now occupied by the W. T. Grant store.

Two of the photographs show special occasions at the Town Hall. Columbus Day 1892 was celebrated as the four hundredth anniversary of the discovery of America, and Main Street was lavishly decorated (**164**). The Saturday matinee crowd is gathered on the sidewalk to greet Santa Claus.

163. Vaudeville Poster.

165. Santa Claus, ca. 1930.

164. Town Hall decorated for Columbus Day, 1892.

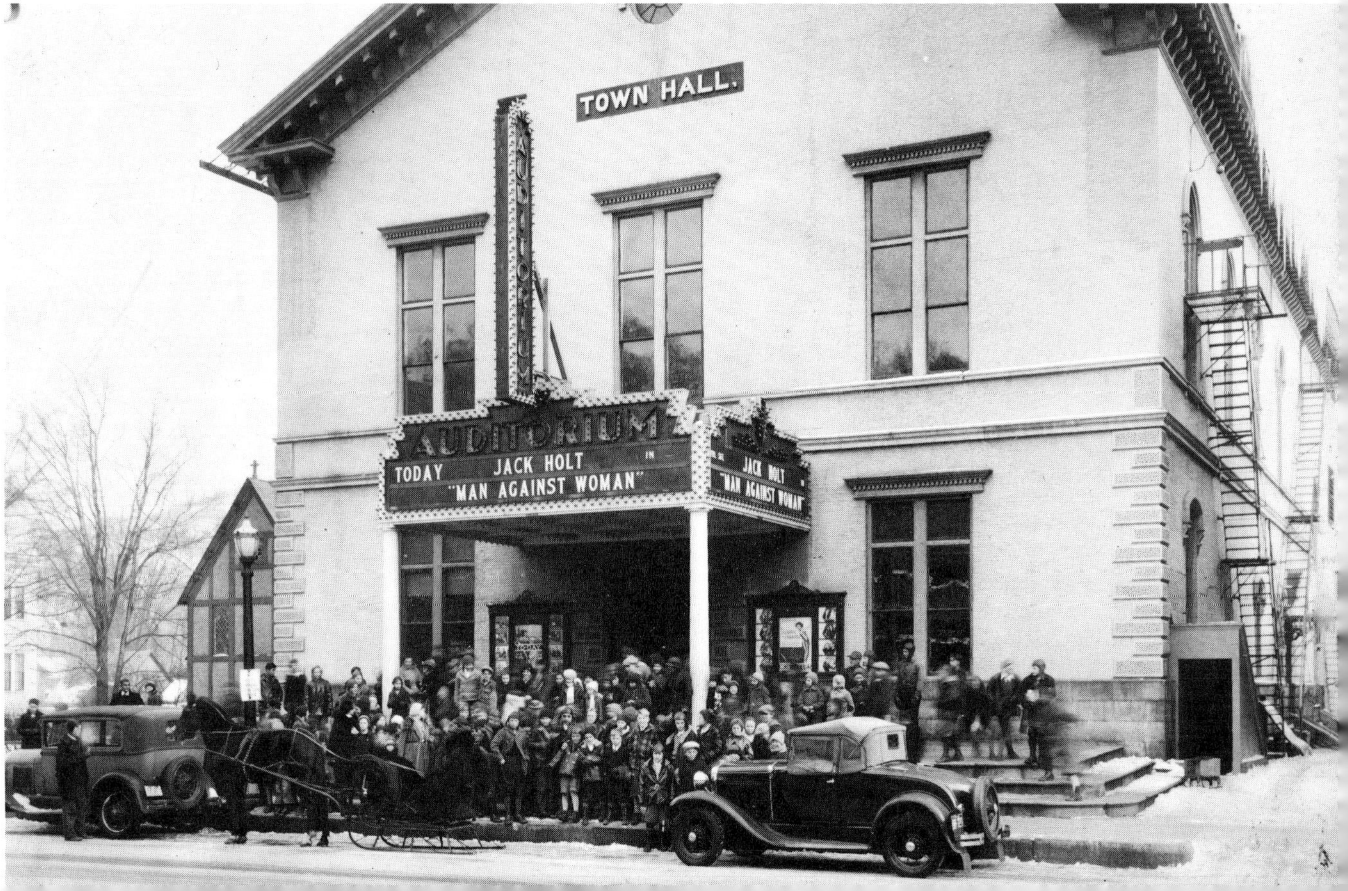

167. Register, September 1870.

166. American House, east side of Main Street Hill, 1880's.

The American House (already seen in **3**) stood on the present Main Street site of the American Building. It is shown here decorated for the Valley Fair: notice the pumpkins, the melons, the Indian corn, the lighted jack-o'-lantern over the door. The commodious porch provided chairs in which a man could sit back, and a stand where he could get his shoes shined.

168. Grand Cavalcade, Valley Fair, October 1891.

169. Suspension bridge dedication, off Putney Road, 1889.

170. Wells Fountain, 1894.

171. Snow roller, Main Street.

A handsome suspension bridge (**169**) carried Route 9 across the Connecticut River from Putney Road to West Chesterfield, N.H. It was dedicated in 1889 and lasted until the flood of 1936. The Wells Fountain at Main and Linden Streets (**170**), completed in 1890, was the work of the architect William Rutherford Mead; it was placed approximately on the location of his brother Larkin's "Snow Angel."

The snow began to fall Sunday evening, March 11. All Monday it snowed harder; the wind blew at upwards of sixty miles an hour. By Tuesday morning, when the storm was over, Brattleboro had received forty inches of snow and the town began to dig out from the Blizzard of '88. Houses were buried in drifts twelve to fifteen feet high. Clearing a passage through the streets (normally a job for the roller, **171**) was a difficult operation. The first path was made by a team of oxen dragging a heavy chain, after which horses could follow. A crew of twenty men was formed on Washington Street to dig a passage to South Main Street; men in other neighborhoods did the same. And the photographer C. L. Howe spent Tuesday taking pictures (**172**)—"picturesque bits of winter scenery," said the *Phoenix*, "which will be of interest for the great-grandchildren of this generation."

172. Blizzard of '88, Main Street.

173.

174.

175.

Country Calendar

100

176.

177.

178.

The changing seasons over the countryside are close enough to be felt in Brattleboro. Plates **173–177** were taken on the Goodell Farm, Sunset Lake Road, West Brattleboro. The gentleman with the beard is Uncle Wes Rockwell, who died in 1915. In the lower picture (**175**) two guests at the farm enjoy a ride on a traverse. Note the use of oxen for haying (**178**) on the Carpenter Farm, off Pleasant Valley Road.

A NEW CENTURY

Looking back, it appears to have been a golden age. The town's industries were thriving, its merchants forever moving to newer and better quarters. Presidents came to speak. Brattleboro had DeWolf Hopper on the stage of its Auditorium—and baseball, dancing, and ice cream at Island Park, a summer resort just across the bridge. The feeling of the era was summed up in the great Brattleboro Pageant. Everybody played his part. There was no doubt that Brattleboro had a lot to be proud of.

179. Memorial Hospital nursing and kitchen staff, ca. 1910.

180. Brattleboro Memorial Hospital, 1920's.

181. Dr. Grace Burnett, as a young lady.

In 1902 the Canal Street estate known as "The Hemlocks" became the site of Brattleboro's new hospital. First called "The Hemlocks Hospital," it was opened as an infirmary for poor seamstresses and shop girls. This was in accordance with the terms of a bequest left by Thomas Thompson, a Boston millionaire who married a Vermont girl, Elizabeth Rowell. Two years later it was decided that the funds from the Thompson trust could be used for the benefit of the public at large, and the hospital was renamed Brattleboro Memorial.

One of Brattleboro's most beloved citizens was Dr. Grace Burnett, a local girl who became Brattleboro's first female physician. Dr. Burnett was born in West Dummerston in 1886 and graduated from Brattleboro High School. She returned to Brattleboro in 1914 and practiced here for nearly fifty years. She loved horses, always keeping five or six at her residence, on the corner of Western and Northern Avenues. Dr. Burnett died in 1963.

182. DeWitt Wholesale Grocery, Flat Street, 1906.

183. Bushnell's store and wagon, Flat Street, 1900.

184. Jason E. Bushnell.

Two familiar Brattleboro institutions of the turn of the century are pictured on these pages. DeWeese P. DeWitt, founder and manager of the DeWitt Wholesale Grocery (**182**), stands at right checking his inventory. Jason E. Bushnell, Brattleboro's most famous grocer, opened his store on Flat Street in 1900 at the age of nineteen. The first day's receipts were eighty-two cents. The old store (**183**) was on the present site of the Ford garage: the young proprietor stands with his arms folded, second from right. Bushnell's moved to Elliot Street in 1915, where its owner began to display his collection of local artifacts and memorabilia, acquired mainly from auctions and attics. In 1946 Bushnell left the grocery business to his sons, bought the Old Red Mill in Vernon, and opened it as a private show-place for his collections. Bushnell died in 1960. The "museum," regarded by many people as the most interesting in the State of Vermont, was destroyed by fire in 1962, along with its entire contents.

185. Main Street, east side, ca. 1917.
186. Construction of Fort Dummer Mills, Cotton Mill Hill, 1910.

Despite several differences, the east side of Main Street as it appeared in 1917 is easily recognizable today (**185**). Automobiles had appeared, but they were outnumbered by horses, and the street cleaner still had a full-time job. The Fort Dummer Mills, Inc. building (**186**) was built on Cotton Mill Hill in 1910. It is now the warehouse and offices of Dunham's.

On Elliot Street around the same time, automobiles have clearly arrived, (**187**). Butter was forty-seven cents a pound at the A & P. Butter was also produced at the Creamery next to Creamery Bridge on Guilford Street (**189**). The bridge still stands, with a covered sidewalk added on the downstream side. Milk was home-delivered, of course: pasteboard milk tickets (**188**) allowed a housewife to pay in advance, then leave a ticket outside the door whenever she wanted milk.

187. Elliot Street, ca. 1917.

188. Milk tickets.

189. Creamery Bridge, ca. 1910.

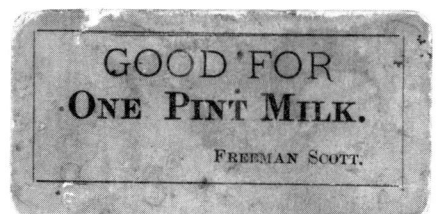

Looking up from Whetstone Falls below Main Street Bridge (**190**), the building at left is the second Brattleboro House, on the site that later became Plaza Park. The building was originally Jacob Estey's second workshop (seen in **61**); it was torn down in 1913. To the right, at the head of Bridge Street, is the building that later became the Hotel Billings. Both buildings are decorated for the Valley Fair. The site of the present railroad station is between Bridge and Vernon Streets (**191**). In the background is the ornate brick station of 1881. John and Robert Manley opened the Brooks House Garage (**192**), in the back of the Brooks House, in 1905. They had one of the first automobile agencies in Vermont, where they sold Hudson and Essex cars for many years. John Ryder's Ford (**193**) was photographed in front of his house on North Street. The view of Flat Street (**194**), looking west from Main, shows Ray's Livery Stables as well as the Carpenter Organ Company.

190. Second Brattleboro House, Main St. Bridge, ca. 1905.

191. Site of the present railroad station, Vernon Street, ca. 1910.

192. Brooks House Garage, 1908.

193. Fall, 1906.

194. Looking west on Flat Street, early 1900's.

195. Barber shop, Main Street, 1907; Clinton Davenport (left) and James Coleman.

196. Richardson's meat market, ca. 1900.

The New Woman

197. The Belles of 1900.
198. Clawson & Hamilton Business School, ca. 1910.

The seven girls at left (**197**) served the refreshments at the wedding of Hattie Marion Jones on June 1, 1900. Occupations available to young ladies were slowly becoming more numerous. Typing classes were given at the Clawson & Hamilton Business School (**198**) in the Grange Block, Elliot Street. Switchboard operators (**199**) were not seen by the public, but nevertheless wore identical uniforms. The World War brought the opportunity of volunteer Red Cross work (**200**); the lady at right, dressed in black, is Mrs. Julius Estey.

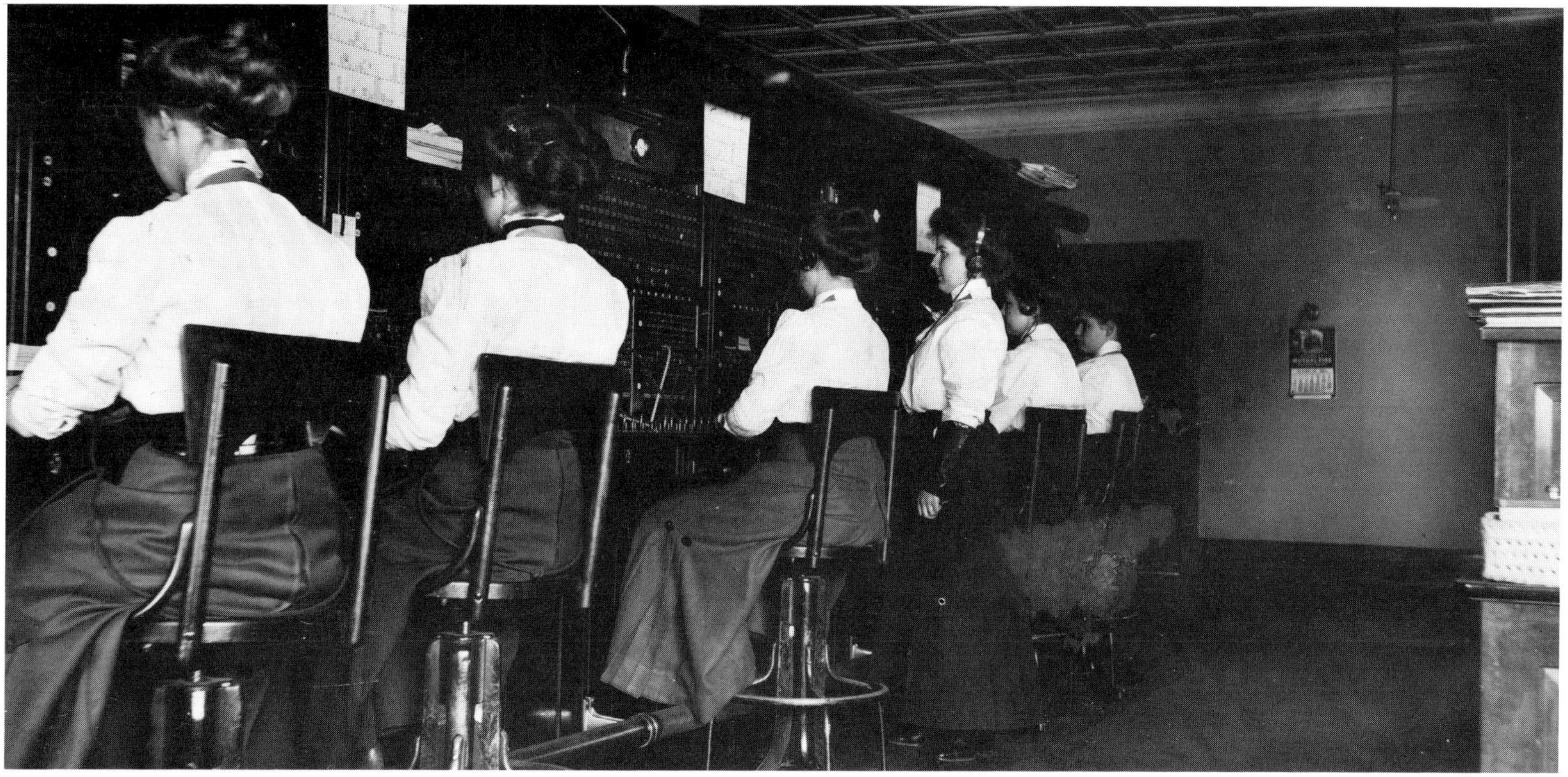

199. Telephone exchange, ca. 1905.

200. Red Cross workers, World War I.

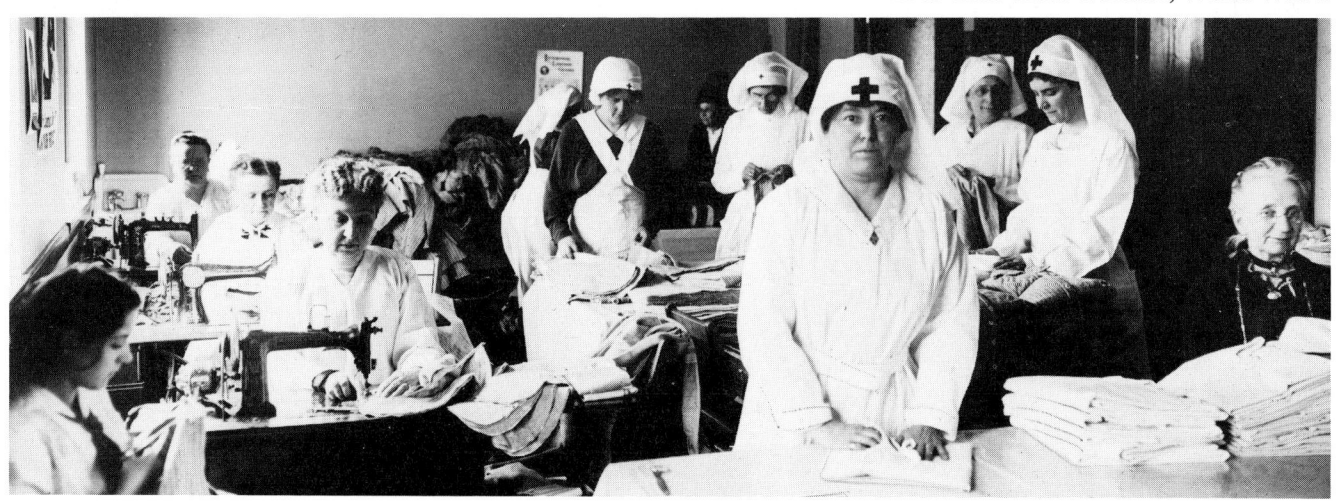

201. Main Street decorated for the Valley Fair, 1900.

202. President William McKinley, 1897.

203. President Theodore Roosevelt, 1902.

The Valley Fair was an annual excuse to decorate Main Street with every available flag. On two occasions near the turn of the century, the flags were brought out for a special event: a visit and address by the President of the United States. President McKinley made a speech on the Common in 1897. President Theodore Roosevelt spoke in the same place (but from the new bandstand) in 1902.

204. Sleigh ride, Green Street, 1900.

205. Ice harvest, Frost Place, 1904.

Winter months brought unique pleasures—including sleigh rides—and a unique industry: harvesting ice for iceboxes. The picture (**205**) shows an ice harvest at the Crystal Springs Ice Company on Frost Place. The ice was sawed into neat blocks then stored in ice houses, packed in sawdust. It kept well enough to provide plenty of ice cream for the Fourth of July. The lady with the hat, the long dress, and the pikestaff is probably Mrs. Fremont Hamilton.

Ready About October 10, 1873.

The Great Literary Sensation.

THE MYSTERY OF EDWIN DROOD.

Completed by the Spirit Pen of

CHARLES DICKENS,

THROUGH A MEDIUM.

Opinions of the Press on Published Extracts.

From the Boston Traveller, July 28.

"Since last Christmas the medium has been at work steadily and assiduously, producing a work which resembles Dickens so closely as to make one start, as though hearing the voice of one long silent in the grave." "The style, to the very minutiæ of chapter headings, is thoroughly Dickensian. If Mr. Charles Dickens had written the work, we should say that he had inherited his father's ability and manner to a greater degree than the heir of any other literary man with whom we are acquainted."

From the Hartford (Conn.) Times.

"It is almost equally remarkable, whether one regards it as a literary fraud, or a real manifestation of some of the mysteries and puzzling phenomena of Spiritualism. One thing is apparent: the quoted extracts from the ghostly second volume do, undeniably, exhibit many characteristics of Dickens as a writer."

From the Worcester West Chronicle.

"Not only surprising talent, but much flavor of the real Dickens wine, is apparent in these communications. * * Enough has already come forth from the pencil-point of this Spiritualist to awaken the liveliest interest and curiosity, and the public will await further receipts with high expectation."

From the Nashua (N. H.) Telegraph.

"The captions of the new chapters are given in full by the UNION, and among them are the following, which are certainly in Dickens' happiest vein. * * * Copious extracts are also given, which all admirers of Dickens will be compelled to confess are not unworthy of his pen."

From an Indianapolis (Ind.) Paper.

"This medium has written, in a semi-unconscious state, a book much larger than the fragment published, and has not only taken up and manipulated the existing characters, but has introduced several new ones—some of them decidedly 'Dickensy.'"

From the Springfield Union, July 26.

"Each one of the *dramatis personæ* is as distinctly, as characteristically himself and nobody else, in the second volume as in the first, and in both we know them, feel for them, laugh at them, admire or hate them, as so many creatures of flesh and blood, which, indeed, as they mingle with us in the progress of the story they seem to be. Not only this but we are introduced to other people of the imagination, and become, in like manner, thoroughly acquainted with them. These people are not duplicates of any in the first volume; neither are they commonplaces; they are *creations*. Whose creations?"

There are forty-three chapters in the whole Work, (embracing that portion of it which was written prior to the decease of the great author,) making one complete volume of about 600 pages, in handsome cloth binding, and issued from the well-known press of Clark W. Bryan & Co., of Springfield, which is a sufficient guarantee of the superior excellence of its typography.

RETAIL PRICE, . . $2.00.

Can be obtained of all booksellers and newsdealers in the United States.

☞ When not to be had in bookstores, the above Work will be sent by mail to any part of the United States on receipt of price, by addressing

E. J. CARPENTER,

Publishers' Gen'l Ag't, Brattleboro, Vt.

206. Broadside for T. P. James's sensation, 1873.

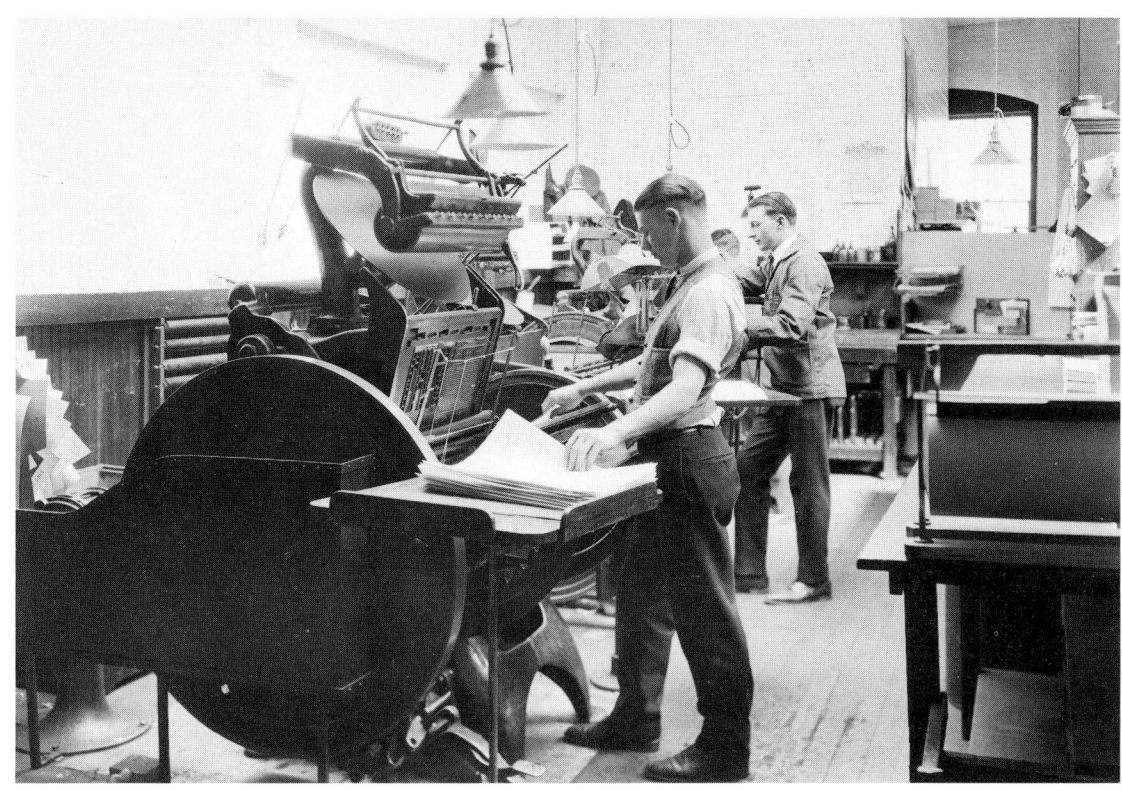

207. Vermont Printing Company, ca. 1920.
208. E. L. Hildreth Company, ca. 1900.

The history of printing and publishing in Brattleboro goes back to the later years of the eighteenth century. In 1920 the Vermont Printing Company (**207**) was doing business in the American Building Annex, where the *Reformer* is printed today. E. L. Hildreth & Company, founded in 1890, was located for many years on Harmony Place. The photograph (**208**) shows the composing room at the turn of the century.

Although Brattleboro has been home to a number of reputable publishers, the most remarkable book published here—and for its time, one of the most successful—was the work of a somewhat disreputable amateur. T. P. James was a tramp printer—a man whose skill with a type case (like those at Hildreth's) enabled him to travel from one town to another, working a while before moving on. In the summer of 1873 it was announced that a man in Brattleboro was completing Charles Dickens's novel, *The Mystery of Edwin Drood,* which was left unfinished when Dickens died in 1870. The man was T. P. James and he claimed that in finishing *Edwin Drood* he was writing from the dictation of Dickens himself, with whose spirit James insisted he was in contact. The project excited much interest, and when Dickens's ghost had done with T. P. James and the finished novel was at last published, there was much fanfare (**206**)

209. Col. William Austine.

210. Austine School, Maple Street, ca. 1912.

211. Alexander G. Bell in Brattleboro, 1914.

The Austine School, which opened in 1912, was founded with a bequest of Col. William Austine, a veteran of the Seminole and Mexican Wars who spent his retirement in Brattleboro. Col. Austine had retired from active service in the U.S. Army in 1862, but he continued to supervise recruitment activities in Burlington and Brattleboro. In October, 1864, he was ordered north with two companies of veterans in response to the Confederate guerrilla raid on St. Albans. He lived in the Brooks House after its construction until his death in 1904. In addition to the money used to establish the Austine School, the Colonel left a fund to the High School, to provide annual awards to the four best scholars in the graduating class. These scholarships, of course, are still in existence.

The famous inventor, Alexander Graham Bell, paid a visit to the Austine School in June, 1914 and spoke at its commencement exercises. He is seen in the back seat of a touring car, driving through town (**211**). The bearded gentleman in front is Dr. Henry Holton, then president of the school.

"The Dying Lion, taken from the original of Thorvaldsen's famous Sculpture at Luzern, Switzerland," was part of an exhibit by Charles L. Gunzinger. The lion was executed in the clay on Mountain Road at the foot of Wantastiquet across the Connecticut from Brattleboro. Mr. Gunzinger's work continued a Brattleboro tradition of ephemeral sculpture begun by Larkin Mead's "Snow Angel."

In the early days of aviation the Retreat Meadow was used as a temporary airfield (**213**). During an aviation exhibit in August 1922, a crash occurred in which three passengers were killed.

212. Lion in clay, foot of Mt. Wantastiquet, ca. 1910.

213. Air field on Retreat Meadow, 1920's.

214. View from Wantastiquet, 1880.

215. Connecticut River bridge and tollhouse, 1880's.

216. Toll bridge corporation shares.

The panoramic view of Brattleboro in 1880 (**214**) makes clear the arrangement of the Connecticut River bridges. The westernmost of the two Island bridges is seen (**215**) looking from the Island toward the foot of Bridge Street. This was the bridge constructed after the 1869 flood, and it was the last covered bridge at this location: it was dynamited in 1903 to make way for a new steel bridge. Until 1888 a toll was levied at the river crossing, and the bridges were administered by a private corporation. On the assumption that people would always want to cross the river, two shares in Hinsdale Bridge Corp. (**216**) probably represented a conservative investment.

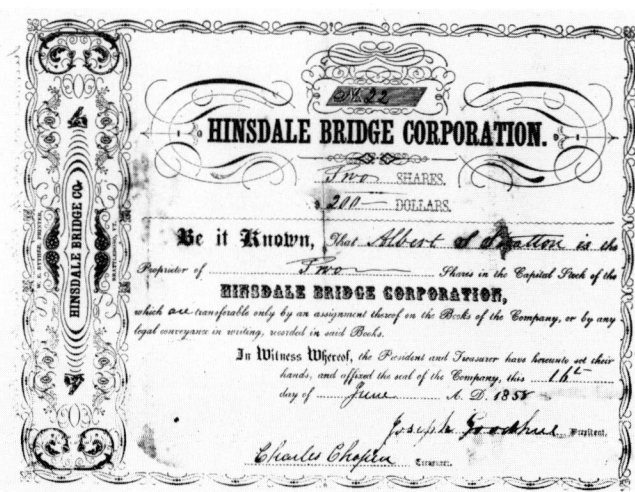

217. Dynamiting the bridge, 1903.

218. Bridge Street entrance, 1903.

By the time the bridge was destroyed in 1903 the roofing had already been removed to reduce its total weight: this revealed the massive laminated arches of the Howe truss construction (**217**). The roofing of the eastern half had been removed first, as can be seen in the photograph (**218**) from the bridge's last days. The "Little River" covered bridge on the New Hampshire side (**219**) was retained until 1928. In 1910, while the Vernon Dam was being constructed, the bridge was raised ten feet by means of huge jacks, set up on blocks (visible at either end). This part of the river was often dry before the dam was completed, and traffic was diverted across the river bed during alterations.

The steel bridge on the West side of the Island was destroyed by flood in 1920. Until the present steel bridge was completed, traffic across the river was carried on a little ferry (**220**) operated by Jack Allen of West Chesterfield, N.H. Two handsome passenger launches, the *New Hampshire* (**221**) and the *Vermont,* served pleasure rather than necessity. Each of these "Bigelow Boats" carried thirty passengers from Island Park to Vernon and Hinsdale (round trip, fifty cents) or on a circuit of the Island (five cents).

219. Little River bridge during alterations, 1910.

221. Passenger launch, 1915.

220. River ferry, 1921.

222. Ice boat, built and operated by Charles Oakes, 1928.

For nearly twenty years, beginning in 1909, Brattleboro's Island—a farm in former times and practically nonexistent today—was a center of diversion and entertainment for the village and surrounding areas. The Island's career as a resort began modestly, with the installation of a ball field and a watering place known as "The Brewery." But these facilities proved popular, and in 1911 the Island Park Company erected a full-scale grandstand for the ball field and an elaborate amusement pavilion (**223**). Here were refreshment rooms (**224**), a ballroom (where Paul Whiteman once played), bowling alleys and a vaudeville stage. Outdoors were frequent baseball games, movies in the evening, and boathouses. Wrestling matches were popular. Circuses would parade on Main Street, then march across the bridge to performances on the Island.

223. Island Park Pavilion.

224. Pavilion soda fountain.

225. Postcard advertisement.

226. Vikings.

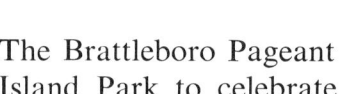

227. The Coming of Art.

228. President William H. Taft, October, 1912.

The Brattleboro Pageant was produced at Island Park to celebrate the 150th anniversary of the settlement of Brattleboro. The Pageant was a lengthy series of tableaux depicting the history of the community. A party of Vikings (**226**) represented the Scandinavian immigration to the village, a troupe of maidens (**227**), "The Coming of Art"—alluding to the work of Larkin Mead and William Morris Hunt. Four months after the Pageant, Island Park saw another special event. President Taft, on his way to a vacation in the White Mountains, was persuaded to stop and deliver an address in Brattleboro. After a lunch with Col. J. Gray Estey, the President proceeded to Island Park, where he spoke for ten minutes from a platform erected in front of the baseball grandstand (**228**).

Among the frequent wrestling matches held at the Island Park Pavilion, the most popular were those featuring George Washington "Farmer" Bailey, the Brattleboro Strong Man. Bailey was born in Cavendish, Vermont, in 1882; he came to Brattleboro as a young man to work in the florist shop of Charles E. Allen. After some years of performing feats of strength for the amusement of his friends—lifting horses, for instance—the "Farmer" made his professional wrestling debut at the Auditorium in 1912, throwing Sandy MacLeod of Claremont, N.H. Farmer Bailey met all the great wrestlers of the day, men like Silent Joe Stecher, Ed "Strangler" Lewis, Stanislaus Zbyszko, Bull Montana, and The Masked Marvel. He was Vermont State Champion, but never attained the World Championship. Bailey retired from the ring in 1928 and went back to work for C. E. Allen. In 1932, aged forty-nine, he tried to make a comeback, but was unsuccessful. He then retired for good, and set up a florist shop of his own on Canal Street.

229.

230. "Farmer" Bailey.

231. Pavilion and grandstand.

232. Baseball grandstand.

233. Pavilion and first steel bridge.

234. Houses on the Island during high water.   **235.** Flooded Island seen from Prospect Hill.

236. The Island Road at flood time.

The attractions of Island Park declined after 1920. People drove their new cars to find amusement elsewhere, abandoning boat rides and outdoor movies. Eventually only the ballroom retained its popularity. But the real enemy of Island Park was the river itself—or rather, the Vernon Dam. After the Dam was finished in 1911, the Island was flooded more or less severely nearly every year. Finally, in the fall of 1927, a flood destroyed the boathouses and left the Pavilion badly damaged. Its owners decided not to repair it, and Brattleboro's pleasure garden was razed.

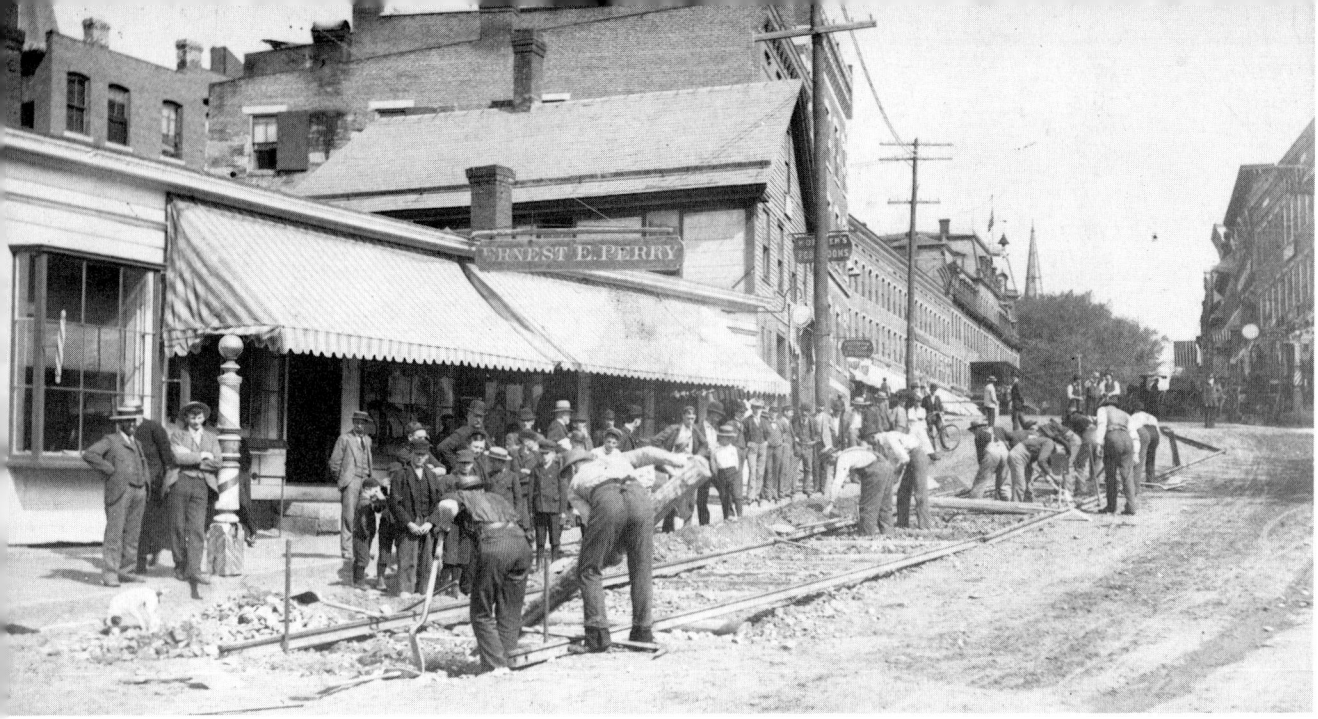

237. Laying the first trolley tracks, May 30, 1895.

239. Trolley tickets.

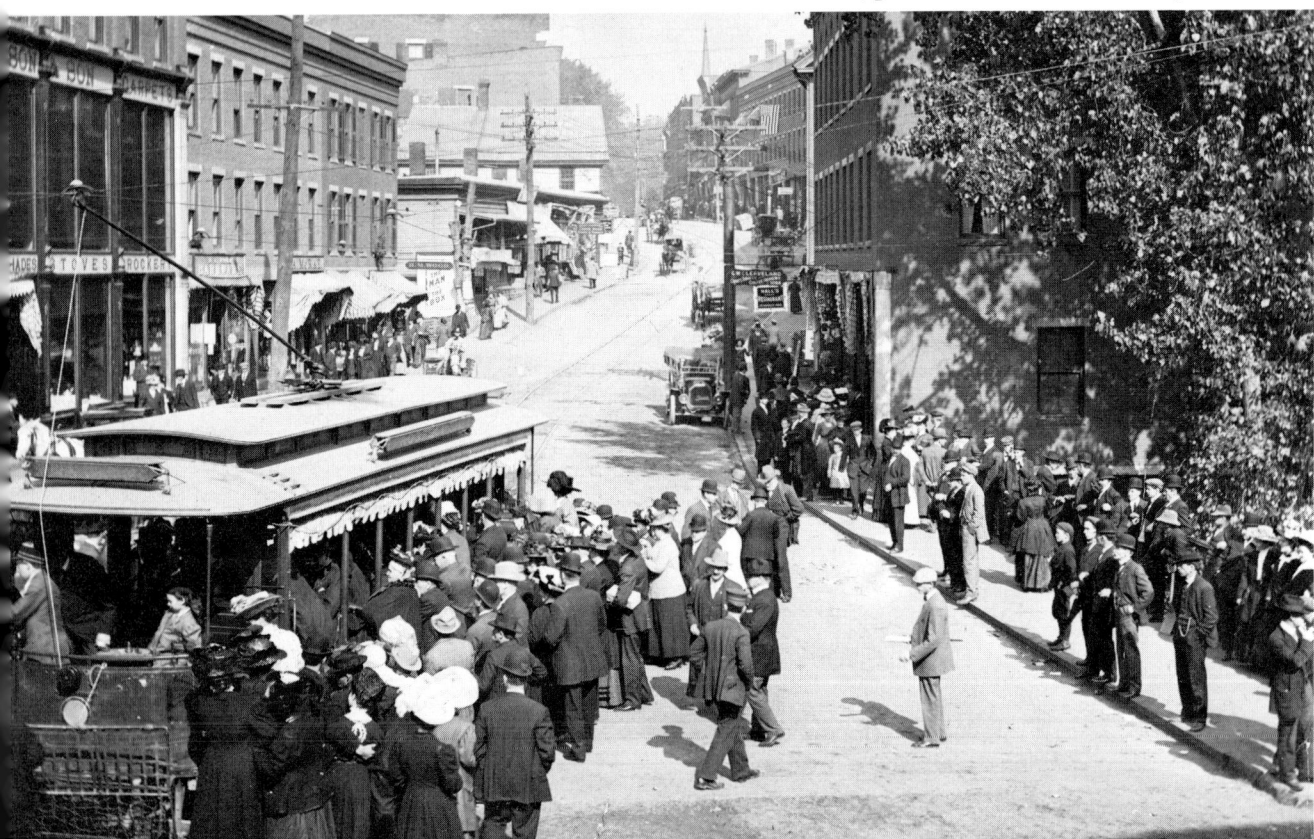

238. "Tickets, please"—Main Street Bridge, ca. 1908.

Public transportation in Brattleboro at the turn of the century was far better than it is today. Backers of the Brattleboro Street Railway Company (E. C. Crosby was prominent among them) finally prevailed over the objections of Rudyard Kipling and others. The first rails for the trolley line were laid on Main Street hill on May 30, 1895 (**237**). The work proceeded quickly and the first cars traveled over the completed lines on July 30th. The route was from Prospect Hill via Main Street to West Brattleboro; the fare was five cents; the cars ran from 6:30 a.m. to 9:30 p.m. The trolley was an instant success: the *Phoenix* reported that "none of the anticipated dangers

BRATTLEBORO STREET R.R. CO.
BRATTLEBORO, VT.
THIS TICKET GOOD FOR ONE SIX CENT FARE
SUBJECT TO CONDITIONS ON THE COVER.
No. 366 E. M. Addi[illegible]
Manager.

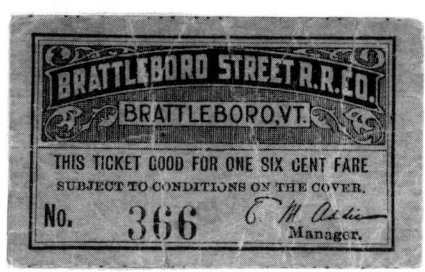

have immediately materialized," and by the end of the year the line was reported to be carrying 2500 passengers daily. The trolleys were abandoned and replaced by busses in 1923.

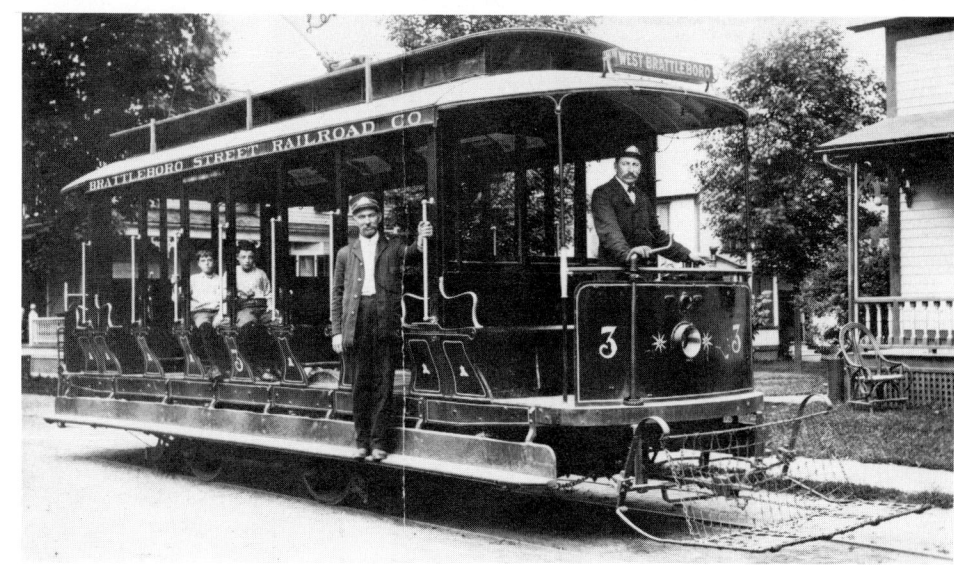

240. Open trolley, 1905.

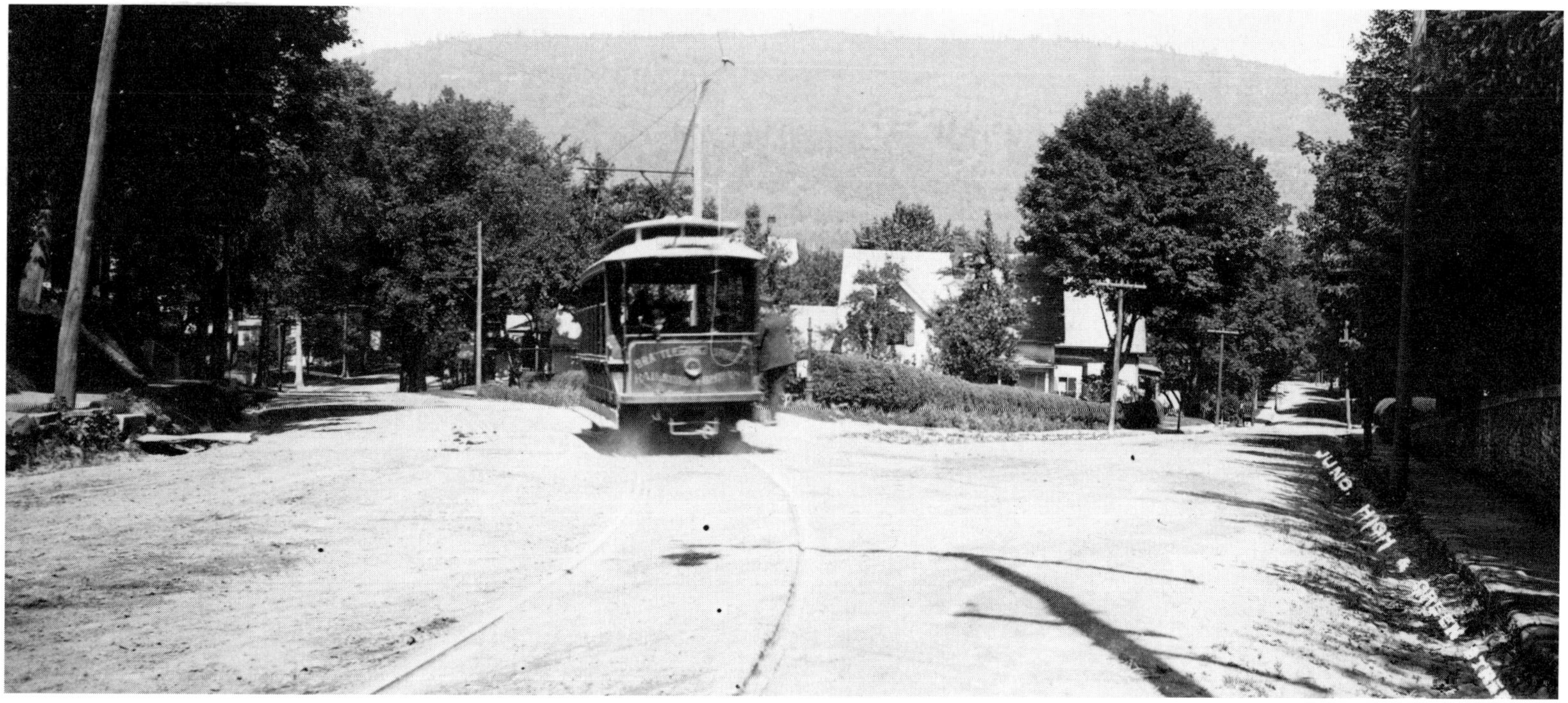

241. Eastbound past the junction of High and Green Streets.

242. View from Walnut Street, 1890's.

243. Working to break the log jam, 1902.

244. Cook's tent, logging camp, 1902.

The easiest way to move logs is to roll them into a river and let them float downstream. From 1869 until 1915—by which time too many dams had been built—there were big log drives every year down the Connecticut River to the mills at Turners Falls and Holyoke, Mass. Near the end, in 1914, 60 million board feet floated past Brattleboro, followed by 30,000 cords of pulp wood. Bridges as well as dams were obstacles to a log drive. In May 1902, a tremendous log jam developed at the old covered bridge to the Island: the entire logging crew gathered to force the logs downstream, and townsfolk watched their labors from the bridge (**243**). Passing through Brattleboro, loggers would camp on the Island (**244**); in the background can be seen the river, solid with logs from bank to bank. Another view of the great log jam (**245**) gives a good view of the old bridge, half-uncovered, in the last summer before its destruction. The round brick building to the right was the gashouse.

245. The great log jam at Brattleboro, May 1902.

Two of the well-remembered men of twentieth century Brattleboro are Pat O'Keefe and Fred Harris. O'Keefe served the town as Police Chief from 1923 to 1930; from then until 1951 he was Sheriff of Windham County. Known to everyone as "Pat," he was especially popular with children and particularly concerned for their well-being. The official arrival of spring in Brattleboro was signalled each year when Pat appeared in his straw hat. He died in December, 1951.

Fred Harris, born in Brattleboro in 1887, was one of the pioneers of winter sports in this country. He introduced ski jumping to Brattleboro and directed the construction of the ski jump at Harris Hill. Harris was first president of the Brattleboro Outing Club, organized in February 1922, and first president of the Eastern Amateur Ski Association, formed the same year. He inaugurated the series of increasingly successful ski meets in Brattleboro that laid the foundation for the modern winter sports industry in this area. Harris died in 1961, having lived to see the post-war boom in skiing as a sport and as a business.

246. Patrick J. O'Keefe.   **247.** Fred H. Harris.

JUST BEFORE OUR TIME

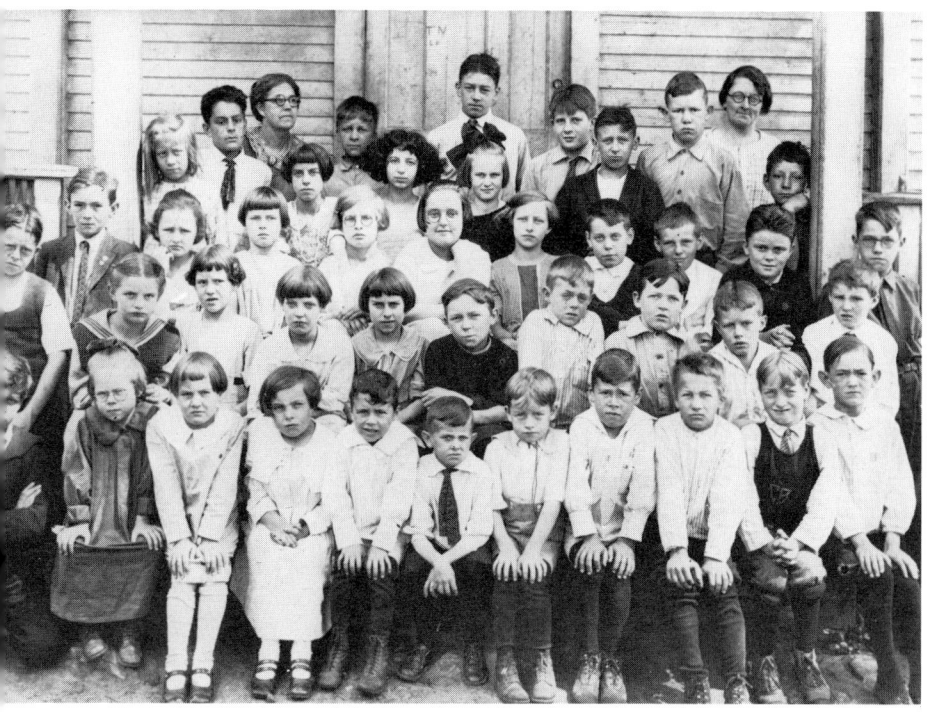

248. Centerville School, 1923.

At Centerville School in 1923 (**248**), children of all the elementary grades were taught by two teachers. A landmark for schoolchildren and adults alike was the candy store on Main Street operated for many years by A. E. Miller. Mr. Miller is shown (**249**) in the candy kitchen in back of his shop, during the 1920's.

249. A. E. Miller in his kitchen.

250. Site of Holstein-Friesian Office Building, ca. 1910.

251. Holstein-Friesian Association of America, 1928.

252. Maréchal Foch, 1921.

The Holstein-Friesian Association, which was to become the largest and strongest dairy cattle breed organization in the world, was chartered in 1885; since 1895 its headquarters have been in Brattleboro. The familiar Association building at South Main and Canal Streets (**251**) was erected in 1917 on the site of Young's Store (**250**). The white building to the right in both pictures is the headquarters of an early fire company. When the building was torn down its bell was purchased by Jason Bushnell. On December 13, 1921, five thousand people filled the Plaza, lower Main and Bridge streets to hear an address by Maréchal Foch, commander of the allied forces in the Great War.

253. Princess Hotel fire, February 1929.

254. Congregational Church fire, 1927.

The Princess Hotel stood at Elliot and Church Streets; the building was originally the Baptist Church and accounted for the naming of the street. By the 1920's the hotel building housed apartments and a theater. The building burned on three separate occasions between 1921 and 1937. After the third fire, it was not rebuilt. A fire at the Congregational Church (**254**), on October 27, 1927, caused extensive damage.

255.

256. Herman Nolin, 1920's.

257. Holbrook station wagon, 1920.

258. Four bridges over the West River, late 1920's.

259. Putney Road bridge construction, 1926.

Transportation in Brattleboro once had a certain variety to it. Mr. Nolin, the mailman, delivered mail with a horse and buggy—and twice a day at that. The Holbrook family could ride to church in the station wagon that Mrs. Holbrook had won in a wartime raffle. (The lady in the second seat, on the far side, is Miss Cabot, compiler of the *Annals of Brattleboro*.) For a brief period in 1929 there were four bridges over the West River (**258**): left to right, looking south, are the main line railroad bridge (still there), the old covered road bridge (demolished soon after the time of the picture), the West River railroad bridge (gone, but the abutments are still visible), and the present-day road bridge. This last bridge is also seen under construction (**259**). And of course, Brattleboro had a working railroad station (**260**). As recently as 1949 there were six trains daily in each direction. Note the earlier station, not yet demolished, and the Plaza, given to the town in 1924 by Lyman E. Holden.

260. Railroad Station and Plaza, ca. 1930.

The crowning glory of life in Brattleboro before our time was the annual Valley Fair. The Fair was held each year from 1886 until the early 1930's, on the fairgrounds off Canal Street, the present site of the High School. The Valley Fair had everything that a fair could have: horse races, agricultural exhibits, rides and souvenirs. It had something more besides—the enthusiasm that the whole town put into the preparations. It was everybody's party.

262. Fairgrounds, back of the grandstand, early 1900's.

263. Ox drawing contest, 1890's.

The Valley Fair welcoming sign for 1908 (**261**) hangs over Bridge Street; note the second Brattleboro House to the right, the Crosby mill to the left. Behind the grandstand at the fairgrounds (**262**) were a number of stands and booths—ice cream, tintypes, both Estey and Crosby firms suitably represented.

261. (opposite) Sign over Bridge Street, 1908.

264. A "tallyho" for the parade, 1890's.

265. "Red Men's" Float, 1895.

The last and best day of the fair began with a parade, starting from the Common down Main Street, then out Canal Street to the fairgrounds. The parade had no end of bands and marchers, but the best parts were the fancy vehicles. As well as the floats familiar today, there

266.

267.

were painstakingly decorated automobiles (**266, 267**) and "tallyhos," a sort of moving pavilion in which young ladies could be conveyed to the fair, and from which they could observe it—above the heads of the multitude (**264**).

268. Diving horse, early 1900's.

269. Harness racing, 1929.

270.

271. Exhibit halls and ferris wheel, early 1900's.

Duke, "the biggest horse on earth" (**273**), was even bigger than Farmer Bailey. He was owned by Charles Miner, who ran the Bonnyvale Stock Farm on Bonnyvale Road: the farm is illustrated on Duke's painted caravan. The horse was exhibited all over at carnivals and circuses, and frequently at the Valley Fair. When Duke died his owner had him stuffed, with a view to continued exhibitions. This relic of the animal ended up at an institution known as Rattlesnake Pete's Museum in Rochester, New York. The museum has since been dispersed and Duke is no more.

Some of the first airplanes seen in Brattleboro (**274**) appeared at the Valley Fair.

272.

273. "Duke," the biggest horse on earth.

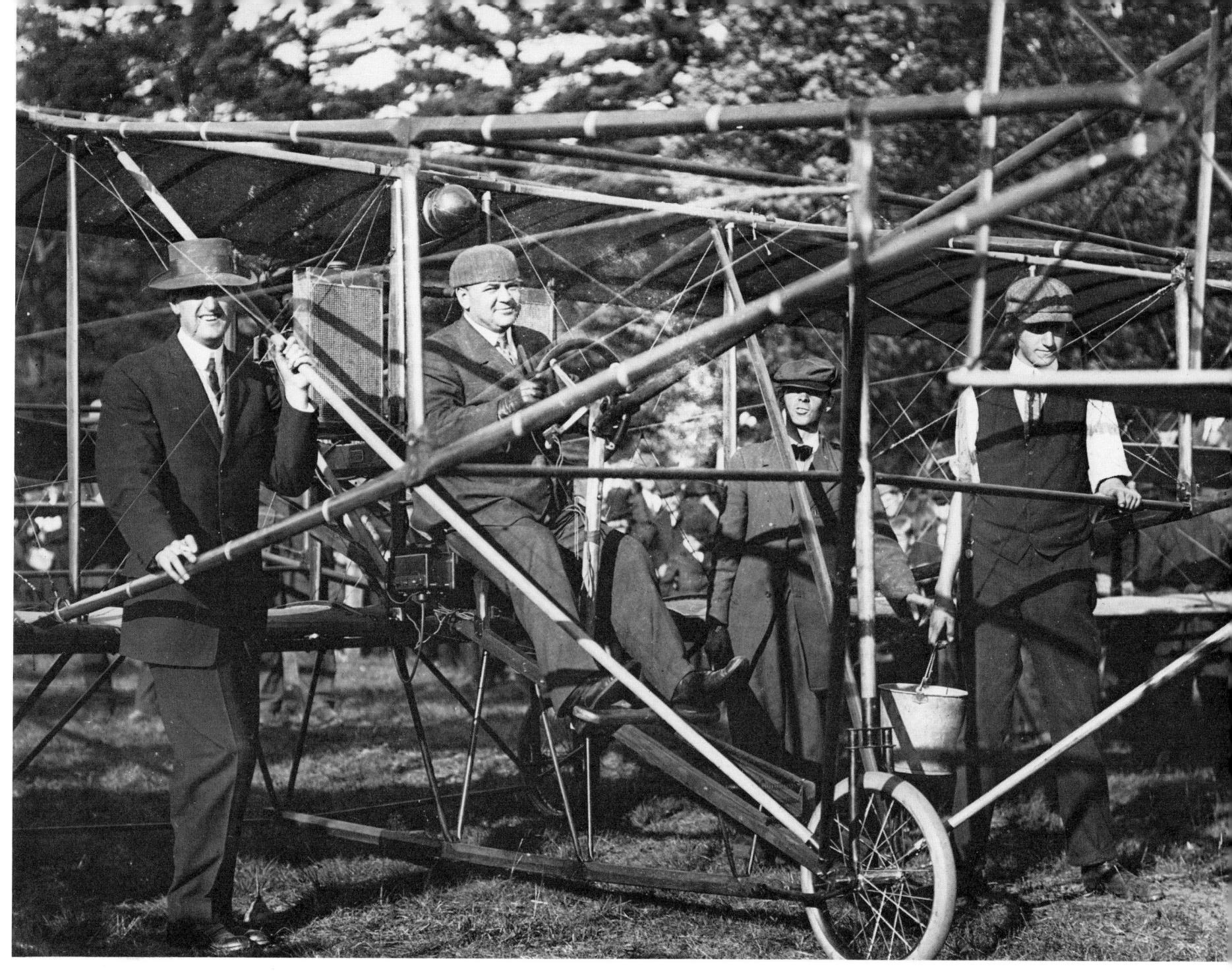

274. An airplane at the Valley Fair, 1910.

275. Auto show, race track, Valley Fair.

More About the Pictures

(Sources and contributors of pictures appear in parentheses, with the names of photographers, where known, in italics.)

Frontispiece. This, the first known view of Brattleboro, looking north over the village from the vantage point of Prospect Hill with the Connecticut River on the right, is from an oil painting done in 1830 by Alvan Fisher. The church tower belongs to the Congregational Church which then stood on the Common. One of the most interesting points about the view is the group in the carryall, foreground—Deacon and Mrs. John Holbrook, their carriage horse, and the family dog are all represented. (Mr. and Mrs. Renouf Russell)

Contents Page. A portrait of William Brattle (1702–1776) by John Singleton Copley. Brattle was one of a group of Boston notables to whom the land that became Brattleboro was granted by the Royal Governor of New Hampshire. He was prominent as a preacher, attorney, physician, soldier, and Tory. The original portrait is owned by Mrs. Thomas Brattle Gannett, of Wayland, Mass., and a copy, now hanging in the Brooks Memorial Library, is the gift of Robert T. Gannett and William Brattle Gannett.

i. Fort Dummer, first permanent British settlement in the territory that became Vermont, was built by the Province of Massachusetts Bay to guard the New Valley settlements to the south. From a 1920's etching by C. J. Brasor based on a 1747 drawing. (Lewis R. Brown, Inc.)

ii. The Arms Tavern was one of the principal buildings of early Brattleboro. The tavern was opened in 1762 by John Arms. Arms was Brattleboro's first postmaster; it is believed that he ran the post office in his tavern. This sketch, presumably based on the remains which stood until 1870, is reproduced from Cabot's *Annals*.

iii. This early map of Brattleboro was drawn in 1810 by Samuel Elliot (for whom Elliot Street was named) to supply up-to-date information to Samuel Whitelaw, State Surveyor-General, for his revised map of Vermont. In the map, "Village Road" corresponds to today's Main Street; "Road to Meetg H. [meeting house]" to High Street; and "River Road" to Putney Road. (Vermont State Archives, Surveyor-General's Papers)

iv. Stone in foreground is that of Samuel Wells, whose epitaph says: ". . . Judge of Cumberland County & a Member of the Assembly of the Province of New York who departed this Life the 6th of August 1786 in the 55th year of his Age." Other early settlers are buried here in Meeting House Hill Cemetery at the top of Orchard Street. Brattleboro's first meeting house was built near by in 1768. (Authors' collections)

v. This stage line served Brattleboro in 1815. (Robert T. Gannett)

vi. Royall Tyler (1757–1826) was a successful Boston lawyer who emigrated to Vermont in 1790, perhaps because his courtship of President John Adams's daughter, Abigail, ended in disappointment. Tyler was the author of *The Contrast*, the first American comedy to be produced in this country. He moved from Guilford to Brattleboro in 1801 and remained here for the rest of his life. In Brattleboro, Tyler served as Chief Justice of the Vermont Supreme Court and as Registrar of Probate for Windham County. Engraved from a miniature now in the possession of the Honorable William Royall Tyler, Washington, D.C.

vii. Deacon John Holbrook (1761–1838) probably did more than any other individual of his time to promote the prosperity of Brattleboro, mainly as a printer and publisher. Holbrook began his Vermont career as a surveyor in the Newfane neighborhood. He went on to interest himself in the business, commercial, educational and religious affairs of the community. (F. Cabot Holbrook)

viii. Mrs. Holbrook was Sarah Knowlton, daughter of Luke Knowlton, an early judge on the Vermont Supreme Court. Deacon John Holbrook and Sarah Knowlton were married in 1786. The portraits of the Holbrooks were probably painted in 1830 by Alvan Fisher, the artist of the Frontispiece. (F. Cabot Holbrook)

ix. In the early nineteenth century, according to a gallows reminiscence entitled "Confession of Michael Martin," Britain was full of the exploits of a highwayman called "Captain Thunderbolt." Thunderbolt was never captured, but disappeared around 1820, to turn up years later as the main actor in Brattleboro's favorite legend. The notorious Thunderbolt, it was said, had fled Britain and started a new life here in Windham County under the name of Dr. John Wilson. Wilson was a schoolteacher, physician, and small businessman of the Brattleboro area. He died at his home here in 1847 and later was identified, correctly or not, as the British bandit of a generation past. (From a portrait reproduced in Cabot's *Annals*)

x. In 1845 Dr. Frederick N. Palmer, the town postmaster, had 400 five-cent stamps printed for use by the Brattleboro post office. In his introduction of a postage stamp for Brattleboro, Palmer (whose initials appear on the stamp) was ahead of the U.S. Government—the rest of the country didn't get official stamps until a year later. This is a late 1800's facsimile reproduction of the Palmer stamp: unused originals sell for $12,000 today. (E. John Bailey)

xi. This lithograph view of Brattleboro from Prospect Hill was drawn in 1849 by M. Stephan, and was printed by Nagel & Weingartner of New York. Clark Street is in the foreground, the Connecticut River to the right. Among recognizable buildings are Reed's Castle, the First Unitarian Church, the Baptist Church (then on Elliot St.), the Gates, Bliss & Co. furniture factory, an early Methodist Church on School Street, American House, and the Centre Congregational Church after it had been moved to Main Street. Town population at the time of this view was about 3,800. (Stephen Greene)

1. This is an 1856 lithograph by J. H. Bufford, published by John Batchelder. (Robert T. Gannett)

2. This picture, from 1853, is the oldest extant photograph known to have been taken of Brattleboro's Main Street. The picture was made by the daguerreotype process, in which a photographic image was produced on chemically treated plates of glass or metal. The foreshortened perspective, which huddles the buildings together in the picture, is characteristic of daguerreotypes. The photographer, J. L. Lovell, came here from Amherst, Mass. Before Lovell, one Elihu H. Thomas, Jr., is said to have made the first daguerreotypes in Brattleboro. Thomas's pictures, however, are apparently lost, and all the earliest surviving pictures of Brattleboro are Lovell's work. Among early photographers in town, Lovell was succeeded by Caleb L. Howe and his sons. (Authors' collections)

3. (George Houghton)

4. Taken from the printer's sample book of George E. Selleck. (Howard C. Rice, Jr.)

5. Dr. Wesselhoeft's residence was a brick house that he built on High Street. The house was later moved to Bullock Street, where it can be seen today. (Mrs. Russell R. Briggs)

6. (*Engraving from drawing by Larkin G. Mead.* Authors' collections)

7. (Authors' collections)

8. (*D. A. Henry.* Authors' collections)

9, 10, 11. (Stephen Greene)

12. Some of the old barracks buildings were later moved

and became houses that exist today. (The *Brattleboro Reformer*)

13. (Robert Knowlton)

14. This picture of Governor Holbrook was taken in his house on Walnut Street. The two other Brattleboro men who served as governors of Vermont were Levi Fuller and Ernest W. Gibson, Jr. (F. Cabot Holbrook)

15. The original part of this building was once the home of Judge Samuel Wells, one of the first settlers in the area, and at one time the owner of most of what is now Brattleboro. Judge Wells built a sawmill on the Whetstone Brook in 1768 and was influential in organizing the first church and the first town meeting. See also **iv.** (F. Cabot Holbrook)

16. After this building was destroyed by fire in 1857, a two story wooden building was built on the site. The later building was lost in the flood of 1869. (Authors' collections)

17. The Brattleboro Melodeon Co. building was later the headquarters of the E. P. Carpenter Organ Co. Still later the C. E. Bradley Corp. occupied the building. The site is now the Flat Street parking lot. (Authors' collections)

18. Early fire companies would "work out" in Frost Meadow. (Dexter Collection, Bailey Library, University of Vermont)

19. Very pretty coin silver spoons, some of which exist today, were cast in this foundry. The site is now occupied by the Brooks Memorial Library. (F. Cabot Holbrook)

20. Mead, later while in Florence, made marble versions of "The Recording Angel," as he then called it. One of these, now in the Brooks Memorial Library, was presented in 1910 to the Unitarian Society of Brattleboro by Henry Kellogg Willard in memory of his parents, Henry Augustus Willard and Sarah Bradley Willard. (*Picturesque Brattleboro*)

21, 22. (Authors' collections)

23. (The *Brattleboro Reformer*)

24. (Stephen Greene)

25. The first bridge to span the Connecticut River from Brattleboro to the Island was built in 1803, the same year that a ledge was dynamited to build Bridge Street. Since then, there have been five wooden bridges and two steel bridges leading to the Island over this side of the river. (Authors' collections)

26. The small building on the left is the Ferdinand Tyler foundry. (Dexter Collection, Bailey Library, University of Vermont)

27. The Hines, Newman & Co. building later became the Stellman machine shop. It was destroyed by fire in 1930. (Authors' collections)

28. The building in the background with the tall chimney was the Woodcock and Vinton paper mill. The Stearns Rule Company (later the Stanley Rule Company) was located in this area. (Authors' collections)

29. (*C. L. Howe*. F. Cabot Holbrook)

30. In 1822, this building was operated as an inn by John R. Blake. It was at this inn, on March 1 in that year, that the first directors were chosen for the Bank of Brattleborough, later to become the Vermont National Bank, now the oldest bank in Vermont. (The *Brattleboro Reformer*)

31. (Authors' collections)

32. Chase's Stage House became the *first* Brattleboro House. The second Estey shop to stand on what is now the Plaza Park (the first shop on this location burned) became the second Brattleboro House, which was torn down in 1913. (The *Brattleboro Reformer*)

33. (Authors' collections)

34. The first and second stories of this building were originally a church in Guilford which was torn down and re-erected on this site. Note the covered railroad bridge over the mouth of the Whetstone Brook. This building existed before the coming of the railroad, and the corner of this building was cut away to allow room for the trains. Barrels of water were kept in the bridge for fire protection against sparks from the locomotives. (The *Brattleboro Reformer*)

35. At the bottom of the mill can be seen part of the old water turbine. (*Lewis R. Brown.* Lewis R. Brown, Inc.)

36. (Hyacinth J. Renaud)

37. (*A. Marshall.* F. Cabot Holbrook)

38. (Brooks Memorial Library)

39. (Authors' collections)

40. This sign is now on display in the Rutherford B. Hayes Library in Fremont, Ohio. (F. Cabot Holbrook)

41. (Howard C. Rice, Jr.)

42. The architect of the Brooks House was E. Boyden of Worcester, Mass. (*A. D. Wyatt.* Mrs. George F. Mosher)

43. (*D. A. Henry.* F. Cabot Holbrook)

44. (Lewis R. Brown, Inc.)

45. (*C. L. Howe.* Authors' collections)

46. (*C. L. Howe.* Howard C. Rice, Jr.)

47. (*F. J. Taylor & Co.* F. Cabot Holbrook)

48. (Howard C. Rice, Jr.)

49. (Authors' collections)

50. Left to right: Elijah Wales, George W. Esterbrook, Alonzo N. Joy, Frederick C. Edwards, Edwin Putnam. (Brattleboro Fire Department)

51. When the alarm rang, horses to pull these Protector Company wagons were brought from Ray's Livery Stable. (Authors' collections)

52. As late as the 1920's, the old Central Fire Station

Fenton's Blacksmith Shop, Main Street, ca. 1890; on the present site of the Ullery block. (Authors' collections.)

Ice company wagons, ca. 1890. (*C. L. Howe.* Authors' collections.)

had its own horses to pull the ladder wagon. The same horses hauled the sprinkler wagon in the summer to lay the dust in the streets. The original station building was altered and is now occupied by the Sherwin Williams paint store. (Authors' collections)

53. (Authors' collections)
54, 55. (Howard C. Rice, Jr.)
56. The residents of Brattleboro raised $25,000 to pay Larkin Mead for the Fisk monument. Lucy D. Moore, Fisk's wife, lived most of her life in Brattleboro. (*Lewis R. Brown.* Lewis R. Brown, Inc.)
57. The Revere House and the Ashbel Dickinson stone building, seen to the left and down the hill, were connected. The second floor of the stone building was the dining room for the Revere House and the third floor was known as "Revere Hall." Town meetings were held there before the town hall was built in 1855. (Authors' collections)
58, 59. (Authors' collections)
60. (Hyacinth J. Renaud)
61. (Brooks Memorial Library)
62. Henry Ford had an organ built by the Estey Co., and came here to visit the plant. He liked what he saw, and sent a personal check to each employee in appreciation. (*C. L. Howe.* Authors' collection)
63. (Hyacinth J. Renaud)
64. (Mrs. Raymond Harrington)
65. (Stephen Greene)
66. To the west of these shops on Birge Street stood the Brattleboro Woolen Mill, at one time owned by Jordan Marsh Co., of Boston. Balmoral woolen skirts were a specialty of the mill. Water power for the Woolen Mill shop came from the mill pond shown on the endpaper maps. In later years the pond provided water power for Holden & Martin's sawmill. (Edward J. Richards)
67. This building, on the site of the present-day Moore Court, was designed for Stoddard by architect Richard Upjohn, and later named "Florence Terrace" for Mrs. Julius Estey. The carriage house on the right served as Brattleboro's Summer Theater for many years. (*Illustrated Atlas of Vermont,* 1876)
68. (Authors' collections)
69. (Dexter Collection, Bailey Library, University of Vermont)
70. (Hyacinth J. Renaud)
71. (Dexter Collection, Bailey Library, University of Vermont)
72. Brattleboro's first railroad station, shown in this picture, was later moved east to the river bank and was for many years the headquarters of Swift & Co. and several other businesses. Although changes have been made in its appearance, it is the original station building. In the foreground is the first of four engine houses to serve the railroads. (Dexter Collection, Bailey Library, University of Vermont)
73. (Authors' collections)
74. (*C. L. Howe.* F. Cabot Holbrook)
75. The high wooden walkway to the left was used to ice the "reefer" cars that carried milk, produce, and other perishables. Ice was harvested on the West River as well as on Frost Place. (Lewis R. Brown, Inc.)
76. (*C. L. Howe & Son.* Authors' collections)
77, 78. (Lewis R. Brown, Inc.)
79. (Authors' collections)
80. (*C. L. Howe & Son.* Authors' collections)
81. (Authors' collections)
82. This house was built in 1759 by Col. Ebenezer Hinsdale using timbers from Fort Hinsdale. (*The Vermont Asylum for the Insane: Its Annals for Fifty Years,* 1887)
83. (*The Vermont Asylum for the Insane*)
84. In 1899 the six hole "Wantastiquet Golf Club" was organized, with its course in the meadow at the foot of what is now Harris Hill ski jump. The present Country Club was laid out in 1913. (*C. L. Howe & Son.* The Brattleboro Retreat)
85, 86. (Authors' collections)
87. (Dexter Collection, Bailey Library, University of Vermont)
88, 89, 90. (Authors' collections)
91. High school football games were at one time also played on Western Avenue where Allerton Avenue is now located. (Brooks Memorial Library)
92. Brattleboro was the second town in the United States to adopt Rural Free Delivery. (Brooks Memorial Library)
93. (Brooks Memorial Library)
94. The mailman here is Spencer Knight. (Harold F. Newell)
95. (Authors' collections)
96. (Harold F. Newell)
97. (Authors' collections)
98. (*W. F. Barnes.* Paul Frizzell)
99. (*C. L. Howe & Son.* Authors' collections)
100. (Howard C. Rice, Jr.)
101. (From Ellis Ames Ballard, *Catalogue . . . of my Kipling Collection,* 1935. Howard C. Rice, Jr.)
102. (From Will M. Clemens, *A Ken of Kipling,* 1899. Howard C. Rice, Jr.)
103. Another popular Kipling work, *Captains Courageous,* was also written at Naulakha. Kipling got the seafaring material for *Captains Courageous* from the experiences of Dr. James Conland, a Brattleboro physician who was a close friend during Kipling's stay here. (Authors' collections)
104. (Authors' collections)
105. (Brooks Memorial Library)
106. (Authors' collections)
107, 108. (Miss Winifred Clark)
109. (*Emery & Wyatt.* Miss Julia Park)
110. This house stands today at 4 Greenleaf Street. (*Henry S. Haywood.* Mrs. Lyman Baker)
111. Note the horse-sweep in the foreground, used to mix the clay for the bricks. (Charles G. Howard, Mrs. George C. Yearly, Harold C. Akley)
112. (*Tri-State Pictorial,* by Charles E. Crane, 1923. Authors' collections)
113. Both Joseph and Francis Goodhue lived in this house. Joseph Goodhue at one time owned all the land on the west side of Main and Linden streets from his house to the Common. (Brooks Memorial Library)

114. Private library societies existed in town before the Brooks Memorial Library. (*A. D. Wyatt.* Howard C. Rice, Jr.)

115. The house on the right was at one time the Uriel Sikes temperance tavern. (F. Cabot Holbrook)

116. The John family have maintained a store in this location for many years. (*Akley & Houghton.* George Houghton)

117. Bliss also designed the Newfane Courthouse. (*C. L. Howe & Son.* F. Cabot Holbrook)

118. (*D. A. Henry.* Mrs. Lyman Baker)

119. This house was at one time owned by Broughton D. Harris, who was born in Chesterfield, N.H., in 1822. Harris graduated from Dartmouth with honors in 1845, and studied law in Brattleboro in the office of Judge Asa Keyes. In 1847 Harris and William B. Hale began publication of The Semi-Weekly Eagle in Brattleboro. In the course of his career, Harris was appointed first Secretary of the Territory of Utah. He was influential in railroad construction all over the United States, and was involved in building the West River Railroad. Harris retired to Brattleboro, where he was one of the original incorporators of the Brattleboro Savings Bank. (*A. D. Wyatt.* F. Cabot Holbrook)

120. The Centre Congregational Church on Main Street is the oldest church building in Brattleboro, but the West Brattleboro First Congregational Church is the oldest organized congregation. This church organization dates back to Meeting House Hill, about 1768. (Authors' collections)

121. The octagon house in the picture stood where Miller Drive enters Western Avenue today. There were two other octagon houses in Brattleboro, both gone. One stood on the corner of Greenleaf Street and Western Avenue, and one on the corner of Putney Road and Terrace Street. (Authors' collections)

122. (*C. L. Howe & Son.* Authors' collections)

123. (Authors' collections)

124. The first house on the left was Mrs. Kirkland's boarding house. (*Akley & Houghton.* Mrs. Alice D. Flagg)

125, 126. (Authors' collections)

127. The old brick house on the left—one of the first brick houses in Brattleboro—was originally the home of the Honorable Jonathan Hunt, Jr., member of Congress and father of William Morris Hunt and Richard Morris Hunt. Jonathan Hunt was the first president of the Bank of Brattleborough, now the Vermont National Bank, which stood on Main Street between what later became, respectively, the Clapp house and the Centre Congregational Church addition. It is thought that both John Adams and Daniel Webster were guests in the Hunt house. The Clapp house, seen at the right, was the first house in Brattleboro to have inside plumbing and central heat. The house was torn down in 1966. (*A. D. Wyatt.* George N. Howe)

128. (*A. D. Wyatt.* T. F. A. Bibby)

129. (*Benjamin A. Crown.* F. Cabot Holbrook)

130. (Howard C. Rice, Jr.)

131. (Authors' collections)

132, 133. Harry L. Emerson was one of the founders of the Emerson Furniture Company. (*With Interest,* Vol. 5, No. 1 [April, 1927]. Vermont National Bank)

134. (Authors' collections)

135. (Mrs. George F. Mosher)

136. (F. Cabot Holbrook)

137. (*A. D. Wyatt.* F. Cabot Holbrook)

138. (*H. A. Smith.* Howard C. Rice, Jr.)

139. (Authors' collections)

140. (George Houghton)

141. (*J. C. Howe.* Mr. and Mrs. John S. Hooper)

142. (Miss Beatrice Vinton)

143. (Hyacinth J. Renaud)

144. The photographer's sign on the Union Block belonged to C. L. Howe. (John Vigneau)

145. (*A. D. Wyatt.* Gustave Westerlund)

146. (Gustave Westerlund)

147. This store was located in what is now the Paramount Theater block. (*Globe Photo Co.* Arthur Scott)

148. (*A. D. Wyatt.* F. Cabot Holbrook)

149, 150, 151, 152. (Authors' collections)

153. (*J. W. Prouty.* Mrs. Gustave B. Westerlund)

154. This picture was taken on Flat Street. The Eddy business later was located on Frost Street. (Mrs. Allan W. Dunn, Mrs. Alice D. Flagg)

155. (*Fred C. Adams.* Howard C. Rice, Jr.)

156. This building burned February 2, 1899. (*Akeley & Houghton.* Mrs. Ralph A. Yeaw)

157. (Authors' collections)

158. (Mrs. John W. Annand)

159. (Mrs. Howard S. Jones)

160, 161. (*A. D. Wyatt.* Authors' collections)

162. (*A. D. Wyatt.* F. Cabot Holbrook)

163, 164, 165. (Authors' collections)

166. The American House was originally built as a warehouse. During the time Deacon John Holbrook owned it, the building was used to store rum and molasses that were rolled ashore from flatboats and steamboats that came up the river from Hartford. In 1840 Daniel Webster was entertained in the American House when he stopped in town on his way to speak in Stratton. The brick building on the left in the picture, probably built before 1818, was torn down in 1924 to make room for the present Richardson Block. (*A. D. Wyatt.* Miss Julia Park)

167. (Hyacinth J. Renaud)

168. The second block on the left (center of photograph), which was located on the corner of Main and

Centerville Store, Western Avenue, ca. 1910; today LaRose's Country Store. (*Bert G. Akley.* Harold Akley.)

153

Silver spoons made at the Burnham Foundry, 1850s. (Authors' collections.)

Flat streets, was torn down in 1936 to make room for the Latchis Hotel. (The *Brattleboro Reformer*)

169. (*A. D. Wyatt.* Authors' collections)

170. Wells Fountain is William R. Mead's only Brattleboro work. Many Brattleboro High School freshmen were initiated in this fountain. (Authors' collections)

171. (*George W. Clapp. With Interest*, Vol. 7, No. 1 [December 1929]. Vermont National Bank)

172. (*C. L. Howe & Son.* Mrs. Lewis W. Prouty)

173, 174, 175, 176. (*Hollis Goodell.* Carl Chamberlain)

177. The string of fish was caught in Sunset Lake (*Hollis Goodell.* Carl Chamberlain)

178. (*Porter C. Thayer.* Mrs. Porter C. Thayer, John Bittner)

179. (Brattleboro Memorial Hospital)

180. Before Brattleboro Memorial Hospital was founded, there were several small private hospitals in various locations in town. (Authors' collections)

181. Dr. Burnett received the Citizen of the Year award in 1961. She was long active in the SPCA. She founded the Green Mountain Horse Association, and was at one time president of the Brattleboro Riding Club. (Mrs. John W. Annand)

182. (William M. Schommer)

183, 184. (Edward B. Bushnell, Mrs. Wallace Foster)

185. Dunham Brothers had a wholesale department as well as a retail shoe store on Main Street for many years. Before the wholesale department was moved to Cotton Mill Hill, it was located in the Hooker Block on Main Street. From small beginnings, this local shoe industry grew to be one of the largest distributors of shoes and Ball Band rubber footwear in the country. (Authors' collections)

186, 187, 188. (Authors' collections)

189. The Creamery Bridge is the only covered bridge left in Brattleboro. It was built in 1879 to replace a bridge that had been destroyed in a flood the previous year. The covered sidewalk shown in the picture was added about 1917. The Creamery Bridge is the only bridge in Windham County with a slate roof. The advertisement on the side of the bridge is for George A. Briggs's store, which occupied premises now used by the Vermont National Bank. (Lewis R. Brown, Inc.)

190. (Authors' collections)

191. The building on the extreme left is the original first railroad station. This picture was taken when Vernon Street (upper right) climbed a hill called "the ledge," which was blasted away in 1914. (Authors' collections)

192. (Randy Wright)

193. Occupants of the car, as of the strollers in **155**, are Howard C. Rice, Jr. and Lyman Adams. (*Fred C. Adams.* Howard C. Rice, Jr.)

194. Ray's Livery Stable burned in 1915 and was replaced by the Barber building. (Mrs. Ralph A. Yeaw)

195. (Authors' collections)

196. (Mrs. Raymond Eames)

197. Left to right: Edith Greene (Mrs. C. R. Aldrich), Kittie Eels (Mrs. Arthur Brasor), Grace Kinson (Mrs. Fred Doak), Amy Jones (Mrs. Howard C. Rice), Florence Thorn (Mrs. A. L. Pettee), Marjorie White and Elizabeth (Bessie) White. (*A. D. Wyatt.* Howard C. Rice, Jr.)

198. The Clawson & Hamilton Business School was a forerunner of the Brattleboro Business Institute, which was in turn a branch of the Bay Path Institute of Springfield, Mass. (Lewis R. Brown, Inc.)

199. (*J. C. Howe.* Walter D. Crossmon)

200. (*Benjamin A. Crown.* Windham County Red Cross)

201. (*Mrs. Charles R. Prentiss.* Mrs. Gilbert Dunnell)

202. (Authors' collections)

203. Theodore Roosevelt spoke on the Common on September 1, 1902, and, on another stopover, at the railroad station on June 7, 1911. (Authors' collections)

204. (Authors' collections)

205. Many years ago this Frost Place business was known as the Brattleboro Ice Co. Later it became the Crystal Springs Ice Co. under the proprietorship of Mrs. Fremont Hamilton. In 1914 the company was purchased by Henry Whitney and Sons and became the Crystal Springs Ice, Wood & Trucking Co. The Whitneys cut cordwood on Round Mountain in West Brattleboro. Their horses plowed sidewalks in the winter. (*George W. Norcross.* Ralph J. Howe)

206. (F. Cabot Holbrook)

207. (*Benjamin A. Crown.* Authors' collections)

208. (Robert L. Dothard)

209, 210. (The Austine School)

211. Dr. Henry D. Holton, the passenger in the front

seat, was president of the Austine Institution from its beginning in 1912 until his death in 1917. Beyond his medical practice, Dr. Holton was well known as a professional man and public spirited citizen. He was president of many local businesses and served on the boards of many Brattleboro organizations. Dr. Holton also served the state and the University of Vermont. (*H. M. Wood. With Interest,* Vol. 7, No. 4 [December 1930]. Vermont National Bank)

212. (Charles H. Gunzinger, Harry G. Anderson)
213. On August 18, 1922, a flight from this airfield ended in tragedy when Evelyn Harris, sister of Fred Harris, and Joseph Trahan and his son lost their lives. Later Ted Reed and Henry Whitney, Jr. developed the Reed-Whitney Flying Service and built an airport on the Putney Road on land now occupied by the American Optical Co. and other industries. (Lewis R. Brown, Inc.)
214. By 1880, when this picture of Brattleboro was taken, the camera had come of age. In spite of the technology then available, however, camera equipment was heavy and cumbersome. The photographer, C. L. Howe, was assisted by his son John, Charles Shattuck and Henry Haywood. The glass wet plate was carried up along with water from the Connecticut River for the developing process. The plate was developed in a black tent on the mountain. (From information supplied by Dr. L. S. Edwards. Lewis R. Brown, Inc.)
215. (*J. W. Prouty.* Authors' collections)
216. (*Prentiss W. Taylor*)
217. (Mrs. Charles Boyle)
218. (*A. D. Wyatt.* Authors' collections)
219. (John R. Wood)
220. (Authors' collections)
221. (*Benjamin A. Crown.* Authors' collections)
222. Charles Oakes (with mustache), a well-known Brattleboro barber, also operated a boat livery on the Island. (Mrs. Joseph Grover)
223. Miss America of 1927 and Miss Universe of 1926 appeared at the Pavilion in 1927. (*D. Roy.* Mrs. Harry Worcester, Hinsdale Historical Society, Inc.)
224. (Miss Julia Park)
225. (Authors' collections)
226, 227, 228. (Howard C. Rice, Jr.)
229. (The *Brattleboro Reformer,* Mrs. Clayton L. Hastings)
230. "Farmer" Bailey stepped into the ring more than 1500 times. Out of his last 1000 bouts he lost only eleven. (Mrs. Clayton L. Hastings)
231. (*Fred C. Adams.* Lyman C. Adams)
232. (Authors' collection)
233. This steel bridge, which washed out in 1920, looked very much like the present bridge except that the sidewalk was on the downstream side. (Authors' collections)
234, 235, 236. (*Fred C. Adams.* Lyman C. Adams)
237. (Richard E. Gale)
238, 239. (Authors' collections)
240. The conductor on the steps is Will Lewis, and the motorman is Elbridge L. Knowlton. Trolley tracks were also laid from Canal Street to serve the Valley Fair. (Robert Knowlton)
241. (*Akeley & Houghton.* C. Kenneth Perry)
242. (F. Cabot Holbrook)
243. (Authors' collections)
244. (Lewis R. Brown, Inc.)
245. (*H. M. Wood.* Walter D. Crossmon)
246. (*Benjamin A. Crown.* Lewis R. Brown, Inc.)
247. Fred Harris graduated from Dartmouth, founded the Dartmouth Outing Club in 1909, and built their ski jump in 1910. In 1913 he published a booklet called *Dartmouth Outdoors,* believed to be the first in America to give instructions on skiing. Fred was elected to the National Ski Hall of Fame in 1957. (Mrs. Fred Harris)
248. Among these students, many of them still residents of Brattleboro, are two of the authors of this book. Can you find them? (*Benjamin A. Crown.* Authors' collections)
249. (Robert G. Ingram)
250. (Paul Frizzell)
251. After Frederick L. Houghton, a Putney farmer, was elected Secretary of the Holstein-Friesian Association in 1894, the Association established its roots in Brattleboro. It was under his leadership from 1894 to 1927 that the Association attained international status. (*Lewis R. Brown.* Authors' collections)
252. (*Floyd E. Johnson.* Authors' collections)
253. (*Lewis R. Brown.* Lewis R. Brown, Inc.)
254. (Mrs. Ralph A. Yeaw)
255. (Authors' collections)
256. (*Lewis R. Brown.* Lewis R. Brown, Inc.)
257. (F. Cabot Holbrook)
258. (*Hayes Bigelow.* Authors' collections)
259. (Authors' collections)
260. The bronze statue "Angel of Life" in the Plaza Park was designed by Daniel Chester French. (*Lewis R. Brown.* Richard E. Gale)
261. (Fred Parker)
262. (Miss Beatrice Vinton)
263. (*C. L. Howe & Son.* Authors' collections)
264, 265. (*A. D. Wyatt.* F. Cabot Holbrook)
266. (Arthur Scott)
267. (Guilford Historical Society, Inc.)
268. (*George W. Norcross.* Ralph J. Howe)
269. (*Hayes Bigelow.* Authors' collections)
270. (Authors' collections)
271. A few of the old horse stalls and other buildings from the Valley Fair still remain and are used by the Department of Public Works. (*Porter C. Thayer.* Mrs. Porter C. Thayer)
272. The girl on the high-wheeled road cart is Susie Randall. (*Jay E. Johnson.* Thomas P. Johnson)
273, 274. (Authors' collections)
275. (*George W. Norcross.* Ralph J. Howe)

Valley Fair prize ribbon. (Authors' collections.)

Chronology

1724	Fort Dummer was built, the first permanent English settlement in Vermont.
1753	Royal grant to the town of Brattleborough was issued by Governor Benning Wentworth of New Hampshire.
1762	Arms Tavern built by John Arms.
1762	The building of Brattleboro proper (the East Village) was begun with the construction of a gristmill at the falls of Whetstone Brook.
1766	Town was patented under Province of New York.
1768	First Meeting House was built, on Meeting House Hill.
1777	The Sovereign and Independent State of Vermont was born.
1784	First post office was established in Arms Tavern.
1791	Vermont became Fourteenth State of the Union.
1795	Samuel Dickinson built Chase's Stage House on Main Street. The first public hostelry in Brattleboro, it later became the first Brattleboro House.
1797	The first printing press in Brattleboro began operation, and Benjamin Smead started publication of the first newspaper, the *Federal Galaxy*.
1804	First Connecticut River Bridge (to the Island) was completed.
1811	First paper mill was built on Main Street.
1822	The first bank building in town was built on what is now the south lawn of the Centre Congregational Church.
1827	The *Barnett*, from Hartford, Conn., was the first steamboat to reach Brattleboro.
1834	Mrs. Anna Marsh left a bequest to found what later became the Brattleboro Retreat.
1843	Dr. Robert Wesselhoeft opened his water cure on Elliot Street.
1846	The Estey Organ Co. was established.
1849	The first railroad to serve Brattleboro pulled into town.
1854	The Town Hall was built.
1856	Larkin Mead created his celebrated "Snow Angel."
1857	Sixteen Main and Flat street buildings burned in a major fire.
1861	Outbreak of the Civil War; Fort Sumter fired on.
1869	A major flood of the Whetstone Brook caused extensive damage. Also this year, fire destroyed all the buildings on the west side of Main Street between Elliot and High streets.
1871	George J. Brooks built the Brooks House, the finest hotel in Vermont.
1878	Construction begun on the West River Railroad.
1886	Brooks Library was established and the library building was built.
1895	A trolley line was laid in Brattleboro; the line ran until 1923.
1897	The first moving picture shown in town, in the Baptist Church.

Other Reading

In the last hundred years, different authors and groups have compiled material and produced books intended to inform the reader about Brattleboro. Not all these books and pamphlets are formal histories, but each of them, in its way, gives a sense of what life was like in Brattleboro in times past. Among these predecessors of *Before Our Time* are:

Atlas of Windham Co., Vermont, from actual Surveys by and under the direction of F. W. Beers, assisted by Geo. P. Sanford & others. New York, F. W. Beers, A. D. Ellis & G. G. Soule, 1869. A reprint in portfolio form was published in Brattleboro in 1969.

Brattleboro, Windham County, Vermont: Early History with Biographical Sketches of Some of its Citizens, by Henry Burnham. Brattleboro, D. Leonard, 1880. This material was compiled by Burnham for Abby Maria Hemenway's *Vermont Historical Gazeteer,* Vol. V, and issued separately.

Brattleboro, Vermont: Illustrated by Autoglyph Prints, W. P. Allan, Gardner, Mass. Negatives by C. L. Howe & Son, Brattleboro, Vt. [1884]. An album of 29 views.

Gazeteer and Business Directory of Windham County, Vt., 1724–1884, compiled and published by Hamilton Child. Syracuse, N.Y., Printed at the Journal Office, 1884.

The Attractions of Brattleboro, Henry M. Burt. Brattleboro, D. B. Stedman, 1866. Second edition, Brattleboro, Leonard's Steam Printing House, 1885.

Brattleborough in Verse and Prose, compiled and arranged by Cecil Hampden Howard. Brattleboro, Frank E. Housh, 1885.

The Best Place On Earth, "Published on Behalf of Humanity at Large by Griggs & Perry, 'The Honest Real Estate Men.' " Brattleboro, 1893.

Picturesque Brattleboro, Rev. Frank T. Pomeroy, editor. Northampton, Mass., Picturesque Publishing Co., 1894.

A Monograph on the Origin and Early Life of Brattleboro, Rev. Lewis Grout. Brattleboro, Press of E. L. Hildreth & Co., 1899.

Brattleboro, Vermont: its attractions as a home, its advantages as a center of business and industry, Brattleboro Board of Trade. Brattleboro, Davenport & Ullery, [1887].

Brattleboro, Vermont—Souvenir, 1912: "The Brattleboro Pageant," Brattleboro Board of Trade, 1912.

Brattleboro, Vermont, A Prosperous New England Town, Brattleboro Board of Trade. [1920s].

Annals of Brattleboro, compiled and edited by Mary R. Cabot. Brattleboro, E. L. Hildreth & Co., 1921–22. A two volume work covering the period 1681–1895, Miss Cabot's is the outstanding book on Brattleboro, indispensable to any investigator interested in the period of the *Annals*. The treatment is in great detail, especially on the subject of early Brattleboro families. A supplementary volume of typewritten notes is available at the Brooks Memorial Library.

With Interest, Charles E. Crane, editor. Brattleboro, Vermont People's National Bank, 1922–32. This is a series of forty-three booklets published by the bank about six times a year. Each issue dealt with a particular topic in Brattleboro history. The *With Interest* booklets are interesting especially for their valuable pictures.

The Geology of the Keene–Brattleboro Quadrangle, New Hampshire and Vermont, George E. Moore, Jr. Concord, N.H., State Planning and Development Commission, 1949.

Pen-drift: Amenities of Column Conducting, by the Pen-drifter, Charles Edward Crane. Brattleboro, Stephen Daye Press, 1931.

36 Miles of Trouble: The Story of the West River RR, by Victor Morse. Brattleboro, The Book Cellar, 1959.

Twenty-five Years of Book Cellaring as recalled by Stephen Greene. Brattleboro, The Stephen Greene Press, 1973. With "a parade of Brattleboro bookstores" from 1795 to 1972.

Brattleboro—Selected Historical Vignettes, John N. Houpis, Jr. Brattleboro Publishing Co., Ltd., 1973.

Files of the annual town directories and of the local newspapers may be consulted at the Brooks Memorial Library.

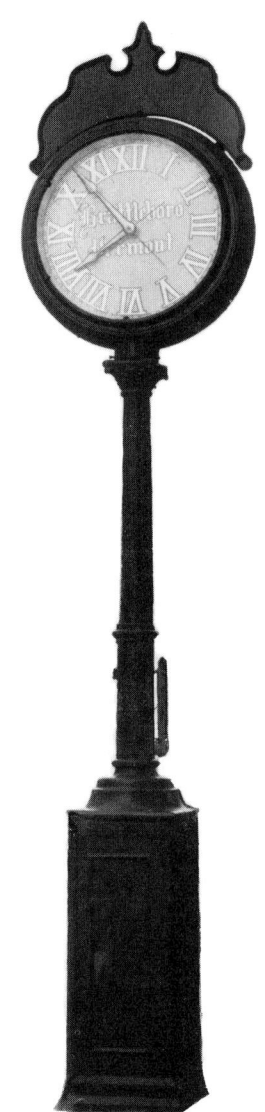

Main Street clock, installed in 1908. (Authors' collections.)

Index

Figures in lightface are page numbers; those in boldface are picture numbers.

Adams, Lyman, 91, **155, 193**
Allen, C. E., 78, 127
   residence, **123**
Allen, Ethan, 15
American House, **3,** 19, 96, 153, **166**
"Angel of Life," 155
Arms, John, 15, 150
Arms Tavern, **ii,** 150
Auditorium, 95, **162**
Austine Prizes, 118
Austine School. *See* Schools
Austine, Col. William, 118, **209**
Aviation, 119, 146, **213, 274**

Bailey, George W. ("Farmer"), 127, 155, **230**
Bank of Brattleborough, **30,** 151
Baptist Church. *See* Churches
Bell, Alexander Graham, 118, **211**
Berkshire Mill, 106, **186**
Bickford Knitting Machine Mfg. Co., **36,** 41
Bigelow boats, 122, **221**
Billings Hotel, 108, **190**
Birge Street, 56, **66**
Blake block, **30,** 37, 39, 44, 151
Bliss Farm, 78
Bliss, Mrs. Minnie, 90, **153**
Bliss, Capt. Nathaniel, 76
Blizzard of 1888, 99, **171–2**
Bond's Undertakers, 86, **145–6**
Bond, William H., 86
Brattle, William, 5, 12, 150
Brattleboro High School. *See* Schools
Brattleboro House
   first, **3,** 19, **25, 32,** 39, 151
   second, 108, 151, **190, 261**
Brattleboro Hydropathic Institution. *See* Water Cure
Brattleboro's Island, **25,** 32, 34, 125, 129, 132, **223–4, 231, 234–6, 244**
Brattleboro Melodeon Co., **17, 27,** 150
Brattleboro Outing Club, 134
Brattleboro Pageant, 126, **225–7**

Brattleboro Reformer, 80, **130**
Brattleboro Retreat, 25, 27, 64, **83–8**
Brattleboro Steam Laundry, 92, **157**
Brattleboro Street Railway, 71, 130–1, **237–41**
Brattleboro Woolen Co., 152
"Brewery," the. *See* Brattleboro's Island
Bridges
   Connecticut River, **8,** 19, **25–6,** 34, 121–2, 132, 151, 155, **214–15, 217–19, 233, 243–5**
   Creamery, 106, 154, **189**
   Island. *See* Connecticut River
   "Little River." *See* Connecticut River
   Main Street, 15, **16,** 27, **29,** 34, 108, **190**
   railroad, 34, 60–1, **73, 76,** 150
   suspension, 98, **169**
   Western Ave., 75, **108**
   West River, 138, **258–9**
   Whetsone Brook, **27–9,** 33
Bridge Street, **8,** 23, **261**
Brooks, George Jones, 44, 76
Brooks House, 40, **42,** 44, 47
Brook House Garage, 108, **192**
Brooks Library, 29, 76, **113**
Buckner house, 83, **135**
Buddington & Brother Mill, **8, 34,** 41
Burnett, Dr. Grace, 103, 154, **181**
Burnham Foundry, **19,** 29
   spoons cast at, 154
Burnside Military School. *See* Schools
Bushnell, Jason E., 105, **184**
   collection of Brattleboreana, 136
Bushnell's Store, 105, **183**

Cabot, Mary R., 138, **257**
"Captain Thunderbolt." *See* Wilson, Dr. John
Carpenter Farm, 101, **178**
Carpenter Organ Co., 108, 150, **194**
Centerville Mill, **35,** 41
Centerville Store, 153
Central Fire Station. *See* Fire Stations

Centre Congregational Church. *See* Churches
Chase's Stage House, 39, 151
Chestnut Hill, 82, **137–8**
Churches
   Baptist
     Elliot St., **xi, 17, 27,** 137, 150
     Main St., 52, 78, **100, 127**
   Congregational
     Main St., **xi, 22,** 31, 78, **127,** 137, 150, 153, **254**
     West Brattleboro, 78, **120,** 153
   Methodist, **xi, 41, 44,** 150
   Unitarian, **xi,** 150
   Universalist, 78, **122**
Church, J. A., Woodworking Co., 93, **160–1**
Circuses, 66, **89–90**
Clapp residence, 68, 78, **127**
Clapp & Jones Bookstore, **148**
Clark Tavern, 76, **112**
Clawson & Hamilton Business School. *See* Schools
Congregational Church. *See* Churches
Creamery Bridge. *See* Bridges
Crosby block, 40, **43, 44, 45, 47, 47, 49**
Crosby, Edward, **46,** 47, 130
Crosby Mill 47, **48, 261**
Crowell, George, 82, **136**
   residence ("Lindenhurst"), 82, **135**
Crystal Springs Ice Co., 116, 154, **205**
Culver block, 19, 30, 31. *See also* Van Doorn building
Cune residence, 76, **115**
Cutlers/Exchange block, 31

DeWitt, DeWeese, **182**
DeWitt Wholesale Grocery, 105, **182**
Dickens Charles, 117
Dickinson building, 53, **57, 59,** 152
Dickinson, Frederick Zelotes, 78
   residence ("Sandanona"), **128**
Dowley residence, 78, **126**
Dunham Shoe Store, 106, 154
"Dying Lion," the, 119, **212**

Eddy, C. H., Bottling Works, 90, **154**
Elliot Street, **5, 17,** 20, 27, **41, 43,** 44, **49, 52,** 106, **187**

Elm Street, **18, 28**
Emerson, H. L., **132,** 153
Estey Guard, 68, **97–8**
Estey, Jacob, 53–5, **62**
Estey, J. Harry residence, 58, **68**
Estey, Julius J., **62**
   Mrs., **200**
   residence ("Florence Terrace"), 58, **67,** 152
Estey Organ Co. (J. Estey & Co.), **16, 18,** 27, 28, **28,** 34, 54–6, 59, **60–6, 69–71,** 91, 150, **156**
Esteyville School. *See* Schools
Exchange block, 23, 31

Fairgrounds, 140, **262**
Farr, Lovell residence, 76, **116**
Fenton's Blacksmith Shop, 151
Ferry, Connecticut River, 122, **220**
Fire Companies, 48, **50,** 136
Fires
   Centre Congregation Church, 137, **254**
   October 1869, **31, 33, 33,** 37
   Princess Hotel, 137, **253**
   Revere House, 53, **59**
   September 1857, 27
Fire Stations, 49, **51–2**
First National Bank, 80, **130**
Fisher, Alvan, 2, 150
Fisk, Col. James, Jr., 51–3, **54**
Fisk, James, Sr., 51–3
Fisk Monument, 29, **56**
Flat Street, **18, 28,** 108, **194**
Floods
   1862, **25,** 32, 34
   1869, **24, 26–9,** 32–4
   1927, 129, **231–6**
"Florence Terrace." *See* Estey, Julius J., residence
Foch, Maréchal Ferdinand, 136, **252**
Football, 66, **91**
Ford, Henry, 152
Fort Dummer, **i,** 12, 150
French and Indian Wars, 12
Frost Mansion, **18, 28, 28,** 34
Frost Meadow, **18, 28**
Frost Place, **205**
Frost Street, **18, 28, 158, 160**
Fuller, Levi K., 55, 85, **139, 141**
   residence ("Pine Heights"), 140

159

Gates-Bliss & Co., **xi**, 150
Gibson, Ernest W., Jr., 151
Glenwood Ladies' Seminary. *See* Schools
Goodell Farm, 101, **173–7**
Goodhue, Francis, residence, 78, **125**, 152
Goodhue, Joseph, 76, 152
    residence, **113**
Gore, John, 41
Grange block, 49, 81, 112, **134**
Green Street, **41**, 44, **204**, **241**
Gunzinger, Charles L., 119

Hampshire Grants, 13
Harris, Broughton D., 153
Harris, Fred H., 134, 155, **247**
Hayes, Rutherford, 43
Hayes Tavern, **39**, **40**, 43
"Hemlocks, The." *See* Hospitals
Highland Park, 82, **137–8**
High Street, **241**
Hines Hill, 82
Hines, Isaac, 82
Hines, Newman Machine Shop, **27**, 34
Hinsdale Bridge Corp., 121, **216**
Hinsdale, Capt. Ebenezer, 152
Holbrook, Frederick, **14**, 17, 25
Holbrook, Deacon John, **vii**, 25, 76, 150
    Mrs., **viii**
    residence, 76, **119**, 150
Holbrook, Rev. John Calvin, 76
    residence, **119**
Holstein-Friesian Association, 136, 155, **250–1**
Holton, Dr. Henry D., 154–5, **211**
Hooker, Corser & Michell, 90, **153**
Hospitals
    Brattleboro Memorial, 103, **179–80**
    "Hemlocks, The," 103
    U.S. Military (1863), 25, **12–13**
Houghton, Frederick L., 155
Howe, C. L., 69
Howe, Mary, 69, **99**
Howells, William Dean, 21, 29
Hunt residence, 78, **127**, **129**, 153
Hunt, Jonathan, 153
Hunt, Richard Morris, 42
Hunt, William Morris, **37–8**, 42
Hyde, Warren, 23

Ice Company, 152
Indians, 11

Island Park. *See* Brattleboro's Island
Island. *See* Brattleboro's Island

James, T. P., 117

Kipling, Rudyard, 70–1, **100–3**
    residence ("Naulakha"), 70, **103**
Kirkland's Boarding House, 78, **124**, 153

Latchis Hotel, 18, 28
Lawrence Water Cure, **6–7**, 21
Libraries. *See* Brooks Library
"Lindenhurst." *See* Crowell, George E., residence
Logging, Connecticut River, 132, **242–5**

McKinley, President William, 115, **202**
Mail delivery, 67, **93–4**
Main Street, 2–3, 17, 19, **19**, 21–3, 29, **29**, 30–1, **31**, 78, 106, **127**, 144, 150, **159**, **168**, **171–2**, **185**, **201**, **237–8**
Main Street Bridge. *See* Bridges
Manley Brothers Garage. *See* Brooks House Garage
Mansfield, Josie, 52, **55**
Marsh, Mrs. Anna, 64
    residence, **82**
Marsh's Brickyard, 75, **111**
Mead, Larkin G., 28, 51
Mead, Larkin G., Jr., 17, **20**, 28–9, 51, 98, 150. *See also* "Snow Angel," the
Mead, William Rutherford, 28, 98
Meeting House Hill, 15
Methodist Church. *See* Churches
Miles, Charles, 27
Miller, A. E., 135, **249**
Moor, Fairbank, 15

"Naulakha." *See* Kipling, Rudyard, residence
Nolin, Herman, **256**

Octagon House(s), 78, **121**, 153
O'Keefe, Patrick J., 134, **246**

Pavilion, 129, **231**, **233**. *See also* Brattleboro's Island
Photography, 7, 44, **44**, 155
"Pine Heights." *See* Fuller, Levi K., residence
Plaza Park, 55, **61**, 138, **260**
Post Office, 67, **92**, 150

Princess Hotel, 27, 137, **253**
Printing Companies
    Vermont Printing Co., 117, **207**
    E. L. Hildreth & Co., 117, **208**
Railroads, 60–2, **72–4**, **77–9**, 81
    West River, 59, **77**
    wrecks, 61, **75–6**
Railroad Stations, 60, 62, **72**, **78**, **80**, 108, 138, 154, **191**, **260**
Raymond, Charles, 23
Ray's Livery Stable, 28, 108, 154, **194**
Red Cross, 112, **200**
Reed's Castle, **xi**, 76, **118**, 150
Retreat. *See* Brattleboro Retreat
Retreat Meadow, **213**
Revere House, 3, 19, **31**, 37, 51, 53, **57**, **59**, 152
Rice, Howard C., Jr., 91, 108, **155**, **193**
Richardson's Market, **196**
Rockwell, "Uncle Wes", 101, **173**, **176–7**
Roosevelt, President Theodore, 115, 154, **203**

St. Albans Raid. *See* Austine, Col. William
"Sandanona." *See* Dickinson, Frederick Zelotes, residence
Schools
    Austine, 118, **210**
    Brattleboro High, 66, **95**
    Burnside Military, **15**, 27
    Centerville, 135, **248**
    Clawson & Hamilton Business, 112, 154, **198**
    Esteyville, 96
    Glenwood Ladies' Seminary, 72, **104–5**
    West Brattleboro Academy, 72, **104**
School Street, **41**, 44
Scott & Jones Grocery Store, **147**
Skiing, 134, **247**
Smith & Hunt Co., 91, **156**
"Snow Angel," the, 17, **20**, 29. *See also* Mead, Larkin G., Jr.
Stagecoaches, **v**, 3, 19, 39, 150
Steamboats, 15
Stockwell, "Aunt Sally," 75, **109–110**
Stokes, Edward, 51

Taft, President William Howard, 126, **228**

Telephone Company, **199**
Thompson residence, 76, **115**
Thompson, Thomas, 103
Town Hall, 68, 78, 95, **97**, **127**, **164–5**
Trolleys. *See* Brattleboro Street Railway
Tyler Foundry, **26**, 151
Tyler, Royall, **vi**, 150
Tyler & Thompson Hardware Store, 23

Union block, 30–1, 88, **149**
Universalist Church. *See* Churches
U.S. Military Hospital. *See* Hospitals

Valley Fair, 88, 96, 115, 140–8, **149**, **166**, **168**, **190**, **201**, **261–75**
Van Doorn, Anthony, 19, 27
Van Doorn building, **2**, **16**, **21**, **29**, **145**
Venter's Brook, 15
Vermont National Bank, **49**. *See also* Bank of Brattleborough
Vermont Phoenix, The, 80, 130
Vermont Wheel Club, 49, **52**, 81, 98, **132–3**, 169
Vernon Dam, 122, 129
Vernon Street, 191
Vinton, John, 23
Vinton's Paper Mill, 85, **143**
Vinton, Timothy, 85, **142**

Waite, Silas M., 80
Walnut Street, **124**
Water Cure, **4–7**, 17, 20–1
Webster, Daniel, 153
Wells Fountain, 98, 154, **170**
Wells, Samuel, **iv**, 15, 150, 151
Wentworth, Benning, 13
Wesselhoeft, Dr. Robert, 20–1, 150
Wesselhoeft Water Cure, **4–5**, 20–1, 29
West Brattleboro, 72–5, 100, **106–8**, 111
West Brattleboro Academy. *See* Schools
Western Avenue, **106**, 108
Whetstone Brook, 15, **18**, **26–8**, 27–8, 33–4, **190**
Willard's Store, 47, **47**
Williston & Tyler Hardware Store, 23, 28–9
Wilson, Dr. John ("Captain Thunderbolt"), **ix**, 150
Woodcock & Vinton Paper Mill, **28**, 151

Young's Store, 136, **251**

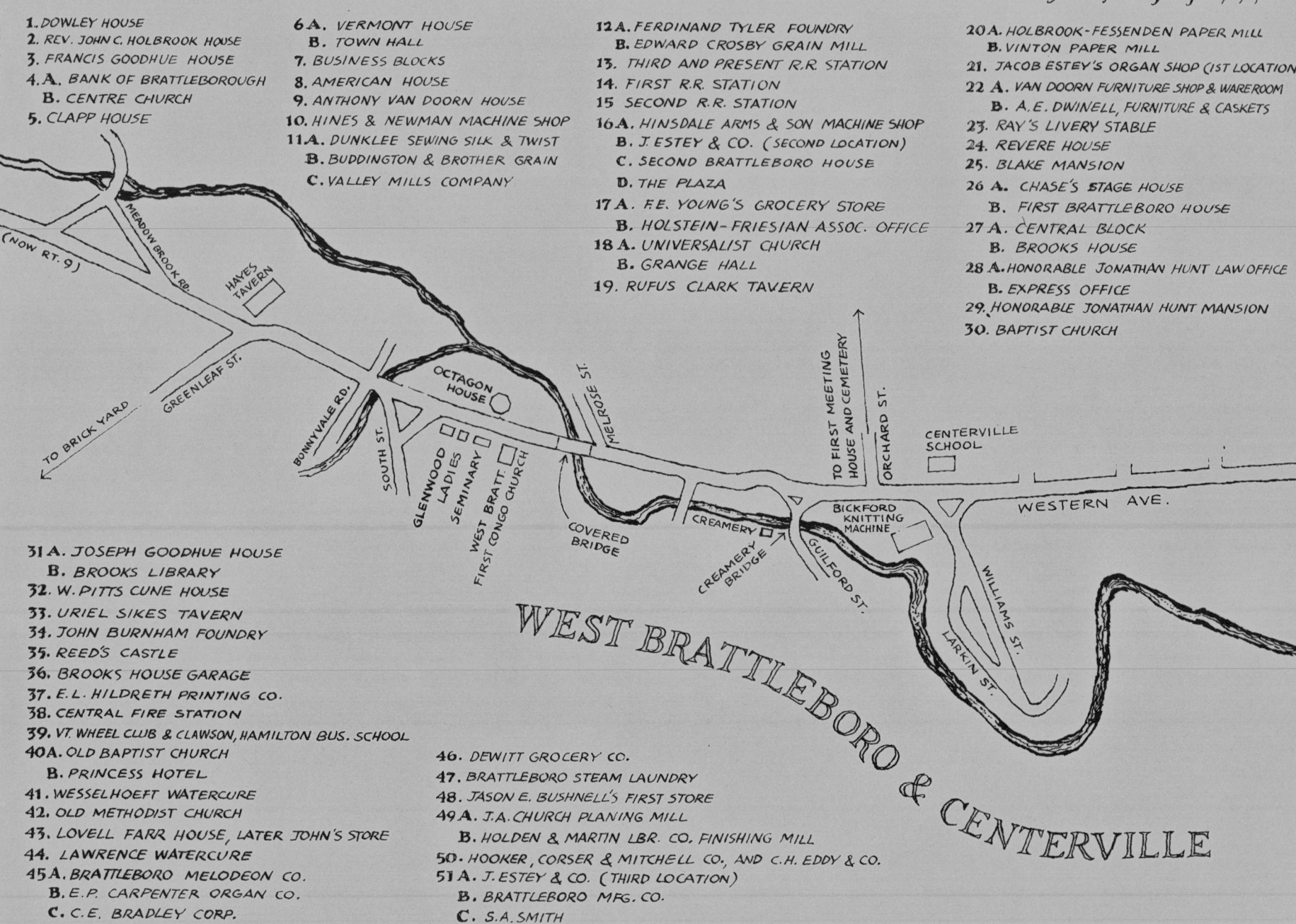

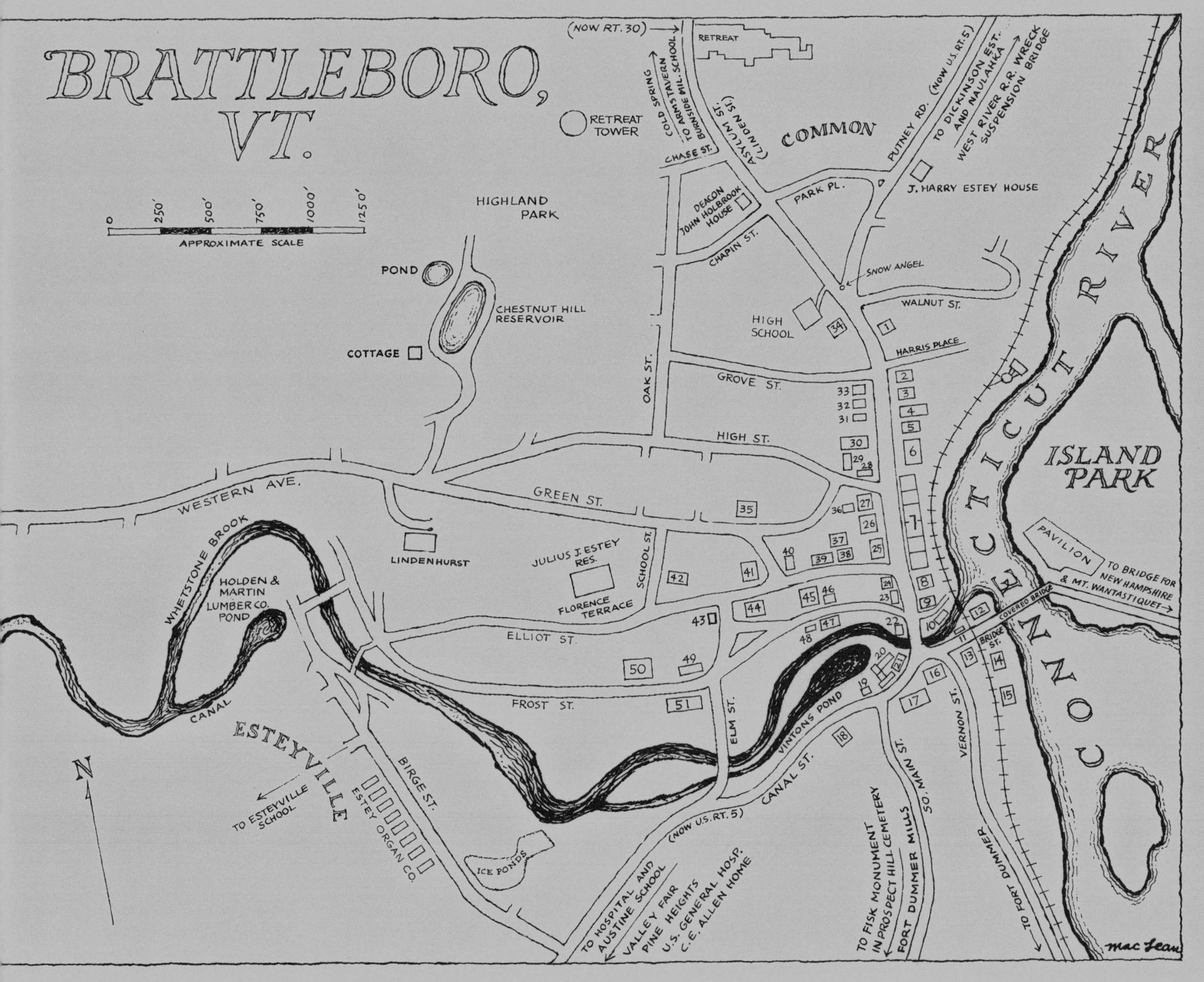